The First True Therapist

By Peter Colla

A Physical Therapist's Journey and Conversations with God, seeking the True Nature of Healing as Demonstrated by the Life of the First True Therapist;

Jesus Christ

THE FIRST TRUE THERAPIST

ISBN: 9781791673994

THE FIRST PURE THERAPIST

THE FIRST TRUE THERAPIST

THE FIRST TRUE THERAPIST

CONTENTS

Acknowledgments

PETER J COLLA

THE FIRST TRUE THERAPIST

ACKNOWLEDGMENTS

I would first like to thank God for the unfathomable blessings He has given me my whole life, today, and forever, as well as the honor of speaking into the lives of His precious children with my own feeble attempts to aid in their own healing process. I would like to thank my wife Anna, truly the muse in my life when it comes to examining, understanding, lifting up, and expressing all the creative gifts God has given me, she is the embodiment of love and beauty being a driving force of inspiration to me every moment since the day we met. Finally, I would like to thank the many teachers and mentors such as Peter Laue and Garvey Graves, who have inspired me to always seek God, especially in the health care environment. They, among the countless others, whom through their own search for truth, real healings, and treatments, discussions of faith and sacrifice could be recognized not only in these pages but also in the written accounts of the greatest healer to ever be spoken of; Jesus. It is in the eyes and testimonies of the many hundreds of people I had interacted in my own healing education throughout my whole life, that these truths were revealed.

THE FIRST TRUE THERAPIST

Introduction

Looking out the windows of light, a person cannot but possibly see all that is in the moment of this reality, the new ventures, the unwanted adventures, the white untouched canvas of an unexpected realization; there is so much out there yet to discover, there is a complete and wonderful creation waiting to be discovered on the other side of this pending voyage. A single day has the potential energy of eternal discovery for every child who opens their eyes, all presented in an unfathomable order of seemingly random perfect orchestrated hues, designed to stimulate senses and ultimately demonstrate the infinite grandeur of a Master Composer and Artist; God.

So was one such day, so are many such days, but are they all not just the same when corralled by the then responsibilities, and the ever encompassing functions that surround a regular day? A morning awakening, its ritual coffee with its own chronic need to attend to that schedule we have so feverishly attached ourselves, giving yet another day in the long list of calendar rehearsals as they play so solemnly past the ever never-ending march of soldiers following in-step, they do so eagerly form the one before another pressing forward, always mindful not to halter from the ones behind, stepping on, in silent but rhythmic procession, keeping step in their ever-present procession, the routine set down before them by powers not quite understood and seldom fathomed.

A person can find themselves on such a journey sometimes hardly knowing the ship has sailed, little do they know they have inadvertently stepped aboard, an unaware stowaway wondering onto valiant voyage destined for distant shores yet unknown and undiscovered. I think such a day was also for me in those such days because in and around the sets of days broader expanses of realization, for they began to find their way into the subtle dispositions of my mind. I guess I was on a journey to discover health, maybe healing, no, truth.

Existing in the health care profession, as many would tell you, especially after years of practicing, the stream of people coming through the door, all with their eyes wide in expectation for what; an answer, a little tidbit of information, one that may lead to ease of burden, a reduction of irritation, the subtle elevation of burden carried by them, in this present and clear torment the irritation of the storms journey has presented them thus far? And what, can you give them, anything you haven't given to a hundred, maybe a thousand others prior to these, regardless of the situation or structures of the facilitator that brought forth the issuing event in the first place?

A person finds themselves in such a present model and over the course of so many years merely a provider of regurgitated leaflets of information that vary if anything from one to the other with as little variation as one might see in looking at the difference between an assortment of aspirin pills in a single bottle. This monogamy starts over time to inflict a more questionable realization in one's heart as to what exactly are you doing here? Are you really helping anyone? And what's the meaning of it all?

In such days, I found myself wondering and asking, if there is more, and if so what?

Still here I am driving down the long morning road, the images playing through the glass as mirages of worlds flowing past like islands across the horizon of some far off sailing soul, one cannot but sometime wonder the worlds of the lives swimming in the lands just out of touch yet passed by each and every day. Do they follow any set path of conversion, or is it just a random dance of unobstructed energy correlating in a pinballs fashion back and forth across a painted canvas frame?

I would like to make a difference, and how can that be, what must I do, to actually be relevant in these peoples lives? A silent prayer, a whim, a hope, a thought dancing just on the surface of another day's morning coffee?

So are the tasks and the course of each day presenting itself also in a never-ending line of people waiting for their rations of the care given them for the injuries that they are rehabilitating from. As so are the task and daily outlook for the therapist who has performed his caregiving duties for last twenty-five plus years?

Such a day, same as many, recognizable as most, no probably all of them, and while the care does change from time to time in a larger scope per particular injury or body part, the regiment is primarily the same and issued out like some meager bowl of porridge to a waiting hungry orphan for another morsel, hoping to relieve that hunger pain or fill some kind of hole left by the tragedy he or she has not quite completely returned to.

So as to find myself wanting a place not common in like, and less desirable then one might think if a more perspective look is examined from afar, wanting in the area of fulfillment, satisfaction as to understanding in one's self, specific to the question; do I really make a difference, am I really helping, seems to be the question? What and exactly is the difference between what I attempt to do, and the actual healing that has been spoken of so often through history and demonstrated with more clarity at least once in history as too; is pure healing really possible and what is lacking to sustain it on a regular and recurring basis?

I have heard it said; "God would that all of us were healed" as well as many other statements that seem to relate to the picture of an ideology that disease like sin, common in many ways is not permanent, and the only thing one needs to be healed from any ailment, is a small yet real formation of faith.

Perplexing thought, given the examinations of many cases in my own mind regarding "The why do some heal and others don't?", this question sits in my head as I ponder the supposition driving down this hill. I have on occasion asked God this very direct and specific question, and most of the time all I seem to receive is the silent quietness that one often associates with a teacher not answering a question in the middle of a lesson because the question has no impact at all on the lesson at hand, or can in itself actually perpetuate more of a distraction from the point being taught if addressed directly.

But I too, have had more of an experience recently with asking and actually have some kind of answer follow, whether by direct word such as something immediately and spontaneously coming out of the radio, or TV, that answers the question, or an image that when recorded or spoken actually solves the question exactly, sometimes, and not as often as I would like, even in almost distinct and all-out audible words playing forth in my head. Today was such a day.

So even as I thought the very thought; "Why do some heal and others don't?", I could hear almost audibly a clear and peaceful response singularly speaking out and drowning out every other sound or even thought, from my head.

"I would that everyone was healed."

I heard it almost as clear as a spoken word sitting right next to me. This understanding of what I had come to know as God's voice, is not as much specific to me as it would seem, just resting softly yet voice specifically inside myself.

There is a deep resonance to it, a voice much like my own yet deeper and older than I have ever heard. There is a peacefulness about it that seems to not only exhibit peace but emanates it in the very moment it is heard. Another interesting fact is, every time I hear the Voice of God all other sounds in the universe seem to suddenly become exceedingly quiet as if only the very sounds that I am hearing, are the only important things I could possibly be concerned with or should be.

Also without really understanding exactly the essence of what I am trying to describe, there is a sort of harmony to the voice as if it is filled with an infinite accompaniment of orchestra or some kind of soft choir just below the surface of my perception. That, and everything I ever hear which appear to be from God is completely different and more comprehensive then anything I may have thought myself, much more wise or simplistic, and seemingly able to cut a perpetual groove into my mind who's memory transcends years, not mere moments, as the many other thoughts or images that flow in or out my head seem to do throughout the day.

So over the course of the next few pages of writing, I will attempt to place those words into some kind of text, some kind of instructional format, passing on the information in essence to others in the same way it was given to me. In some cases to lay understanding to it myself with my own dealings, but also to help others whether caregivers or those in need of care, who also may be struggling with these same questions.

"So if You would that everyone would be healed, what is stopping them, why do only a few seem to be healed?" I asked not exactly expecting an answer. Then the most shocking answer came instantly and unexpectedly.

"They Are!"

Let's Take a Journey?

So began a conversation between myself what I knew was God. Hearing the voice of God seemed not as strange as the words that came as an answer, and the perplexity of the promises spoken.

I clearly heard the spoken words *"They Are!"*, or at least I feel like I did, at least enough to act upon it over the next few years.

I have always been a man who believed in God, and while I believed many of the stories or reports of miracles, healings, or other unexplainable events catalogued or reported from varying and reliable sources, often especially in the area of healthcare, of which I myself a self-proclaimed expert having been a practicing provider for at least thirty nearly forty years, my own faith in the completeness or at least the final authority regarding healthcare options rested firmly within the present system, of which I myself diligently participated, rarely did this with any apparent uncertainty come into question. At least that was when it came to my own opinions or thoughts. Basically, I believed that anything within the western medically taught and accepted-view of the disease and affliction processes, and their possible treatment options, where carved in stone, undisputed or at least when it came to ideas outside the licensed and regulated profession I happen to practice in. Anything that deviated from these bordered on fraud, black magic, or wishful thinking.

So receiving a message, even in my head, that completely contradicted this notion was either from some joking or deceiving subconscious anomaly, of which I could discard as perhaps my own mind playing tricks on me, or perhaps, just maybe, it was God? But I had faith enough, and perhaps a sprinkling of wisdom given me earlier in my years, experiences, and teachings, to know that if it is God, the message would always be verified, repeated, and emphasized to the point where a person cannot help but hear it, if one chooses to turn a deaf ear in the first place.

I seemed to begin a process of "Schooling Up," and while I hardly realized at that particular moment, that school was actually in session, and never really stopped or closed since I never the less took my lesson with all the authority granted any teacher presenting thus far. Maybe that is actually how God does it, gives you a little, and then sees how you handle it, then later after proper digestion, gives you more? Well whether this is how it is with others it is certainly what I observed over the course of the next few or more years, and most probably continuing today.

For the next few months, I initiated various aspects of trial and error applications of the various things God shared with me, pertaining to applying a more faith-based application within the processes of therapy as each seemed to unfold themselves throughout the months and even years to follow.

At various times, small words of wisdom, I would later refer to them as "Gems" would be deposited into my life through examples, spoken words, directly or indirectly, dreams, and visions, always perpetuating in seemingly the same fashion. I would know these Gems were from God because He would distinctly tell me at that moment too; *"Pay attention, something good is coming right this moment!"*

Often the specific significance of each lesson or word wouldn't seem initially to be relative for the specific moment as much as it was just almost supernaturally clear, many having an immediate and almost emotional effect on me, being deposited into my mind over the course of months and even years but for the purpose of this book, as I was and am instructed to write, they all in their right time bubble back up into the surface of my consciousness with amazing clarity.

I will catalog these conversations as chronologically accurate as possible, seeing they developed over ten years. The words I heard or at least knew were directly from God I have written them in the form of *Italics* and put them in quotations because they are not just for me but for everyone who would hear them or use them for their own good.

So the journey starts.

"People are healed every moment of every day, they are from the first morning of the first day they move, whether they breathe a breath, or utter a sound, or form a thought."

"To understand the nature of healing one must first

examine and understand the aspects of exactly what is going on. A person cannot understand, let alone hope to fight a battle such as a sickness if they are looking in the wrong direction or blind to exactly what forces are acting upon them, let alone attack them."

This I understand, we as medical practitioners often try to get at the root of the causes of any and all ailments, what tissue exactly is being affected, what structures are damaged, what seems to be amiss, this is how we treat effectively and not waste time working on things that have no basis in the injury itself.

"This is where you fail, examining the results of an attack on the body, without looking at the actual cause of the attack is no different than treating puncture bites after the snake repeatedly bites you and then slithers off. All you end up doing is chasing the shadow."

"You can not drive out darkness with darkness, and while much of the basis, the original wisdom given to your fathers was good, it has been taken captive by the enemy and laced with darkness with one purpose and that is to enslave, steal, and destroy my children."

We are taught that if we can identify the exact tissue or the basic factor in the body causing the irritation, then we have a greater chance of actually facilitating the correction, we can help heal the patient.

"This is an incomplete form of healing, you are only attempting to heal a small fraction of a person, a mere structure inside of you, not unlike trying to right a single stone in a wall that is falling. You are more than hairs on your head or fingers on a hand, more than bodies, you are also spirits."

"Let us take a journey and I will show you how true healing is achieved to everyone who merely asks, and afterward how Godly therapy should be performed on the aftermath of your affliction, just as I already demonstrated so many times and with so many healers before."

Slavery of Healthcare

"There are certain absolute truths that are promised to all of you equally and completely; first among these God keeps all of His promises."

"This is a primary fact you will need to understand as you examine further the aspects of health care and how My promises are instrumental for setting My children free from the slavery the current healthcare model provides."

I had similar conversations throughout the almost ten years it took to assemble these writings with God. They developed in the form of visions and dreams regarding the true nature of insurance and the spirit behind it, the way people should look at sicknesses they were suffering from, and how to effectively treat them to be healed.

"Sicknesses, injuries and all sorts of infirmities; they are merely shadows cast by the gifts I gave your fathers and

15

mothers over the years."

Slavery in itself is a deplorable practice, and prior to writing this book, one that I felt had been eliminated from society today? But what exactly is slavery other than the unwilling bondage placed upon one individual, active removal of free will to effectively make their own decisions regarding any aspect of their own lives?

If we look at this ideology in a broader sense than just a landowner or even social structure such as a country, then one could broaden the definition to include any institution in which a person's freedom is taken from them for the benefit of another. Modern corporations seem to do this all the time and this is no more evident than in health care.

I would share these words and others moving forwards in their appropriate place and time, but for the time being, will try to stick with health and wellness.

There was a time when people would go to the most learned or experienced members of their community for help with their health care issues, and these people would give them fair advice for fair pay.

I can remember a day early in the career of a health care provider, one with fonder reflection, a gentler time, when basking on touch of soft scented spring breezes felt like willows lacing themselves in the arms of those in need with honeysuckle blossoms, cast their long slender branches into depths of peacefulness, gave way to a view to a calmer reflection of tender gentler care. So was health care of old, or so it seemed.

Men and women soft of touch, yet firm of thought, rendered all types of healing arts with actions of professionalism, given not for prestige or money, even as this most usually and almost assuredly followed, but for the deep desires to merely help other people in need. This very desire being the driving force that released spirits into the sacrifice of reaching out a helping hand, a man could find a special calling, giving a sweeter meaning to life, that without, would most assuredly lack taste or spice, a bland dish; unpalatable.

Even within my own years, especially early in my career people would come in with an air of expectation and more than that, they would have *"Hope,"* woven in the fabric that was the blanket of a medical provider, regardless of title or accumulated letters behind their name, hope that they could actually help them with the issues they suffering from, help them feel better?

To answer such a deep seeded calling, when one could see the life dwelling within the very eyes of the many he or she might help in this world, and perhaps aid through the seemingly impossible trials of sickness and despair, many often brought to some in the form of a quenching water to the dry mouth of life, one merely had to desire or volunteer to the task of helping their brothers and sisters with the affliction these happen to be suffering at the time, to fulfill this calling.

The earliest Nurses were Nuns attached to churches where the sick happen to be brought for care. The earliest Doctors were the learned men or women who happen to be schooled in the known processes of the body, the bio-physiologies, the biochemical and structural components as understood at the time, and within these areas of practiced science specifically understood or practiced the treatments of the injuries presented.

Was it not a simpler time, and not all to long ago, when

people paid for the medical services they needed, a fair price for the time spent, and while I may be giving up my age by saying so, many times people who were even a little short, might bring in eggs or a baby pig, or maybe do a little work on leaking plumbing in the Doctor's basement as a payment in like, and to this medical caregiver; payment of such was just fine!

"Just and Fine" two beautiful statements of truth.

It was the gratitude expressed in the smile of a woman face when she finally came to the realization her child was going to be all right, or the injury to her husband wasn't as bad as suspected. And while the two chickens or newly finished quilt hardly made up for the relief they found, ever happy was she to know that the Doctor, the kind man or gentlewoman, who had been such a Godsend, would sit for many a warm night inside the arms of that quilt it took her so many hours to produce, maybe presenting but a fraction of the warmth her love ones produce for her as well.

But as sudden as a thief in the night the system was overtaken by wolves in sheep's clothing, or so it seemed, specifically in essence by the insurance and pharmaceutical companies. I wrote the following article and posted it on paulorpeter.com February 24, 2014, describing my own realization and the results this takeover of the health care system had on care as a whole. This article as with many others I felt was inspired, prompting me to write it based on images or dreams given to me by God.

"When you wrote those word I was giving you eyes to see the theft within your own practicing environment and how greed allowed this temple of a false god to slither its way into what should have been a noble and caring practice."

It was as sudden as a thief in the night, or maybe a dark mold slowly growing in a dark damp place, whose dark tentacles only show their intent long after the roots sit so far in the foundation, nearly nothing can remove them. A creature of dark-hearted stealth started slithering its evil talons hidden right in plain view, only inches from the bare innocent feet of our children.

Enter the insurance company, the heartless snake, who creeps in with a seemingly innocent statement; "Give us a little of your money each month for medical insurance, so you can be Insured, or ASSURED, that when you have medical needs, the money will be there to help pay the medical bills, the care will assuredly come, we will pay for it and not you!" But that is not exactly what was delivered?

I saw over the course of only twenty or thirty years, first people give away their rights slowly and systematically to the insurance companies. What started out as an agreement to pay, later resulted in the insurance companies deciding exactly how much and more importantly who to pay. They used the payment and media delivered concerns for preventing fraud as a basis for requiring authorization before a person could be treated for anything. Of course, they could never stop anyone from treating if they chose, but they would refuse to pay if a practitioner didn't ask for authorization in advance.

This too was limited later by the same insurance carriers then telling the medical practitioners how much, how often, what medicine or medical procedure they would authorize or not, and the only people who would become aware of the dark controlling enslavement that had occurred were the people who unfortunately fell so fall down the rabbit hole of needing healthcare, they could hardly afford to complain, just take it and just suffer.

"In essence, by taking control of everything when it comes to the children of God, it does result in enslavement by everyone involved."

This does seem to be the purpose and goal of false gods, to completely enslave people. Where first they desire and demand people's first fruits, even deducted from their checks before they have a chance to touch the money they earn, then make them beg to even have a little portion back.

"You must understand the nature of the beasts you are dealing with if you are going to victorious in this battle."

"They want all the gifts and treasures I have freely given to you my children, all of the health, wealth, devotion and thankfulness for everything that is already your, even to the point of your whole body, mind, and spirit."

"It is an institution of slavery, this is the malevolence of the spirit that desires innocents to participate"

The dark spirit doesn't seem to stop there, I have seen most people who are afflicted their every desires, their every thought, delivered waves of stress, anxiety attacks, addictions, worries, pain, and fear always seem to be directed towards or fixated on the issues they are suffering from regardless of how small the area of affliction is, they seem trapped to think about at every moment of the day.

"You must remember the darkness does not have the power to take it away from you that which I have given, for if they could they would. You freely give it yourselves."

"Do not be deceived."

"Freely have I given you all Good things, and only you have chosen to turn your back on me, and walk away from Me and them."

THE FIRST TRUE THERAPIST

Children of the Morning Sun

A dream?;

Many children sit beside the road and are crying, stomach sore and hands aching because they are hungry, and the few bites of food are not satisfying the hunger that is piercing their insides like a sharp sword digging deep into the soft underside of that world which they have called home for as long as they have known.

Hands and feet ache, so much so, that they can hardly walk anywhere else, or use their hands to produce something to trade for more food. And where would they go anyway, there is nowhere apparent they can go for relief, all the teachers are telling them to sit still and drink the drops or dirty filthy liquid, eat the black tar that is laying around? The so-called experts tell them; It is what is done!

These beautiful children just seem to get sicker the longer they sit, and while a few do pop up occasionally and seem to improve, the majority just fall back down, failing from another issue different but unusually similar to the previous one suffered.

A Man, a child himself, who just happens to be looking up notices something on the hill, the mountain off in the not so far distance, he starts a slow climb walking along and even says to a few of the children within earshot, *"Get up and walk up that mountain nearby and drink of that clear brook, eat of the small herb that is growing on the bank, the one sitting quietly in the sun. It looks good."*

Without even knowing how he knows he says without hardly thinking; *"The very food you are eating is causing you to feel the hunger pain, the dark dirty water is making you sick."*

"The fact that you use your hands for the wrong work, collecting the wrong things, is causing them to ache, and your feet are twisted and sore from you sitting on them or walking in your foolishness."

Suddenly and for the few that listen, the pains of the dark sword diminish and the strength of healing flows through their body like the rays of warmth on a perfect summer sun on cold wind frosted skin. Merely by walking in the right direction, life's blood flows back into their feet, color returns, and stiffness with its pain disappears, or did it disappear the moment they started walking?

Hands reach out and help others, help themselves picking up life, in their own soul's journey. Along the way, as they climb even just the foothills they notice springs of clear water flowing with bubbles of freshness from the ground, reflecting light like stars glimmering in a day's bright blue sky, free of the black oils they so often have tasted in the past.

The herbs are everywhere ripe and eager to be picked, their taste a perfected blend of everything they know they need to satisfy the desires of their bodies need. Hunger pains flee! They cup clear cool water to drink, and they become refreshed. Thirst flees! Each experiencing healing the minute they move toward the new direction, the moment they begin in their spirit to start to believe they can actually get better.

Many of the young children run back and tell others of the wisdom they have heard, some even bring the nourishment back. The disease that they all were told was incurable, flees their bodies like cockroaches fleeing when the light is suddenly turned on, and murmurs of despair are replaced with sudden smiles and voices of happiness, hope, and faith.

The children discard the black tar they have clung to for so long, they spit out the filthy liquid they have been told to drink, they know now that healing has rained down upon them from above and silently give thanks up unto the mountain at which their liberation sprung.

"One of the great issues is you have been taught, trained, or even convinced into believing is the false image of who you are, what is your place in this world, and even to the point of being deceived into thinking you are powerless in the happenings that go on around you, especially as they pertain to your health."

"This is perpetuated from almost the earliest age you begin to process memories, and reinforced through every possible source whether it be education, media, doctors, government or leadership, even religion."

"Before you can truly comprehend and effectively deal with what is happening to you in sicknesses and injuries you must understand the truth about the composition of your life and your place in the world."

"If you were to try to put a physical image on people or society what comes to mind?"

When I think about society as a whole or think about a

representation of the people symbolically, it is easy for my mind to go to the symbol of the pyramid on the dollar bill. I have been told this was placed there as a symbol of our society?

"Well, that's a good place to start."

Truth Hidden In the Dollar

Investigators will tell you, that if you want to find the truth and expose the criminal, look at those who are telling the most talking they will inevitably give away the light as they describe the shadow in their darkness.

We are taught that our bodies are everything. The Physicality of where we are right now, exactly how we feel right this moment is pretty much the major aspect of any disease or problem we might face physically.

The essence of any injury can be analyzed and then, if the structures that are injured or affected could somehow be reversed, the issue or disease should disappear as well. Nice thought, makes sense and it pretty much takes the thinking out of any problem. The tumor appears, remove the tumor, problem gone?

Unfortunately as is the case in most issues the problem doesn't seem to disappear but merely reappears later in another spot.

Mind over matter, the power of positive thinking, Law of Attraction, The Placebo Effect, or various other areas of ideology that put power in the mere way we think, have begun to spring up in various areas of the treatment environment, yet it only seems to get the most fringed recognition often being spouted as a sort of heresy, how dare we think we can tell the doctors anything, they know it all, and for the most part fall short of delivering when applied to our specific case?

Belief? Well, forget that, the spirit, that's pretty much for the miracle department, and those examples of miraculous healing only seem to happen to other people, often fabricated or just some miss-diagnosis that someone else completely fumbled.

Maybe this is why injuries have a way of defining our lives?

Speak to anyone who has an injury long enough and you will find that for the most part, people can speak of nothing else than the injury they are dealing with, and more so the symptoms. You can talk about the most relevant thing in the world, and after you finish a sentence, and then go on to ask them about something you have been talking about, they merely revert back to the subject of their own fixation, that issue that is causing them distress in their life!

It is so true especially in healthcare, I have noticed that when people are hurt or dealing with a healthcare issue their "whole world" becomes this issue, and regardless of how actually small, the issue is, the world it is none the less. I have known people who have nothing more than a sore pinky toe, and their entire life seems to revolve around this one particular issue. They only think about the toe, they consider the toe, they look at it, they feel it, they see it, their whole life revolves around it as if it is some sort of dark black hole, and they have suddenly become trapped in its ever constricting and crushing orbit, spinning down deeper and deeper until death itself becomes a mercy. The black little toe hole!

"The injury through fear and deceit cause your eyes, ears, and every thought to dwell on the issue at hand." "Windows are shut or shaded preventing you from looking out onto the world, where the attack stemmed, and where your solution lies."

It does seem in a self-defeating mannerism, to be an almost slave, not unlike worshiping in a zombie-like trance of consideration for the little toe.

"People have a tendency to turn their faces to the ground, the press their face into the muck and their whole world

becomes consumed with the injury."

"They become a slave to the injury, regardless of how insignificant it is in proportion to the whole body, and even greater is the effect on the family or it's resulting waves throughout the entire community."

"But let us get back to the symbol of people as you are taught."

Like I said, I have often believed or may have been taught in my youth that when considering the whole society the symbol of the pyramid on the dollar bill is supposed to represent us as a society in whole. Should we consider the perspectives of this taught view of us, we might even see ourselves as this constructed stone like a pyramid, let us take the one off the one dollar bill as an example?

Our life then becomes a representation of the monolithic simplification of the pyramid, as it seems to be so demonstrated throughout history. Pharaohs, leaders all around the world have used this pyramid structure as a representation or demonstration of the life these many great people, countries, cultures have presented, as a way to represent or "Re-Present".

So let's take the representation of the pyramid; in this model, the body is the huge base covering the mass that rests against the earth, grounded and needing at least the majority of our consideration for anything to continue, unmovable and face down in the dirt?

The mind then would be the middle section, less then the body but sitting above directing the whole comings and goings of the body, visible and aware of its place in the whole picture; above the body, kind of like the mind or head resting on top of the body, the director, the boss?

Well, then what is the spirit? That little all-seeing eye that kind of floats above, small, insignificant, detached, it radiates with some kind of detached power, light, radiation or whatever, and just floats there not really doing anything at all, inconsequential?

If they lie about one thing then are they lying about everything?

"Let us consider the opposite is true."

A sort of reverse pyramid image might appear?

Then the body would actually be the very smallest portion of the whole?

"The physical body is the smallest portion of your soul. The soul is in essence then the entire aspect of your life in this physical life and beyond."

The sharpest and insignificant point actually touches the ground. It expands upward and outward for about one-third of the evident structure. It might in this case and as an example of real people make sense?

Science would tell us that the body is merely a conglomeration of assembled atoms, coordinated in the most complex fashion, so complex that they can hardly understand them to let alone fathom the systems that govern them, yet they are convinced, and it is commonly taught, that all atoms are merely various organized structurally restricted entities of energy, locked in a particular structure and orbits around each other, and further organized in complex patterns that somehow make us up as human, and for the most part the entire visible and invisible universe? Real, now and present for just this one particular moment in time. Not unlike sound waved flowing like the ripples through a pond one moment here and the next touching the edge of the sand.

The mind lets assume, in turn, rests above larger and

growing upward structures expanding, it might make sense seeing how the mind not only encompasses everything in the now, taking all of its stimulus from every aspect the body might offer but also incorporates memory; past present and even to a degree that which we might imagine a future, but also extrapolates this information making judgments as to the effects of the past on present information and a possible projection to theoretical future predictions based on data received to date. A sort of enormous library with shelves for past experiences, interpretation, and reactions to be placed for future reference and deductions.

Then what about the spirit? If it rests above and is the essence of our belief system, it is how we believe, it might make sense that it is a product of everything that the mind processes, all the stimulations the body feels at any one particular time, fed up into the mind, processed along with dreams, teachings, imagination given to us through conscience and even un-conscience stimulus and then passed on to the belief system, the spirit to assemble and collect, building its own collection, as it was, to make our own ultimate decision; deciding ultimately what exactly it actually believes? Does it swing toward yes or no, good or bad, dark or light, God or something else?

If this be the case and the spirit resides up and into heavenly realms of considerations, one might also assume in our structural demonstration that the spirit would go on and upward actually without an end?

So back to health care.

If we are actually structures of not only physicality in the present, but also past present and future and more importantly the mind has a much greater volume of consideration of the whole, then one would and must assume that the spirit has the greatest consideration if for no other reason then the massive volume of the whole it seems to be in charge of.

The first step in confronting and eventually eliminating any medical issue a person may be suffering from on an ongoing basis, it is first necessary to understand the issue at hand and exactly what we are fighting.

Given the fact that we are the greatest proportion of our essence in spirit then we must also realize that anything that happens to us good or bad in our lives is primarily spirit based, and knowing this makes it so much easier to fight and defeat in the case of a negative confrontation.

We have been taught we have little or no influence on the

outcomes of issues that afflict us, that we are some sort of random occurrence and when bad things happen to us it is just Karma, bad luck, or being at the wrong place at the wrong time. But this misconception has the effect of taking the Divine out of our paths and makes us a bit of a slave to whatever infirmity that may present itself. It is so easy with such thought to just give up and not even begin to hope when we are suddenly afflicted with a dreadful occurrence.

The actual specifics of the injuries are too complex to understand and must be left to the people who have been taught these facts. As a matter of fact, we are systematically being taught we should not even question the diagnosis or prognosis when told to us merely act on the results, and do what we are being told.

"Yes you have been enslaved by fear, deception, and false teaching, but when you lift your head up, start to ask for wisdom, I am faithful to give all you will need to overcome any issue you may seek help with."

THE FIRST TRUE THERAPIST

Look for the Signs

"I give every person alive who chooses to look unto the light, signs to show I fulfill my promises; Rainbows, they are My gift to My people as a reminder to them that I always keep my promises. It is no different in healing when people are faced with drastic and dramatic choices you would be amazed how many look to Me when all else seems to fail. I would it that they would look to the light long before the skies become so dark."

It is no different in my own life or the majority of the people I have treated, people, in general, seem to have to hit rock bottom before they are willing to actually make real changes that result in some good and positive changes in their lives. I have to honestly say over the course of my adult life the majority of the greatest and most positive changes in my own life for the better came on the precepts of calamity.

"All thing can be turned to good for those who seek God. It is not different in health, storms or dealing with attacks, it merely presents opportunities for growth, which by the way is every given day in your life."

"Like the rainbow, it is a promise."

"You yourself have seen rainbows of all types when you have been in a place of asking, looking to me for help and then waiting on Me for answers, guidance or help. I gave that gift to men way back when I first gave it to Noah, and I always have and continue today, for those who first step out into the light, choose to follow and look in the right direction?"

How do we know it is the right direction though?

"The majority of people do not look to Me until the situation or issues of the world literally forces them to. All forms of storms, afflictions, attack, or infirmities can be classified into one simple example; children find themselves either by action or directions at one moment of more face down in the muck. When you are face down in the muck there are two choices every individual must choose between; either leave their face in the muck, give up and die, or lift their head up and live?"

"Lifting the head up is lifting it towards God, you are lifting your head up with the choice for life, life is a gift from God and thus you are choosing Me, whether you realize it or not."

"This upward motion represents a desire to live on and not just give up. Lift your head, look up to Me and you are taking the first step onto the path of healing no matter what affliction you are suffering from."

I have seen it in patients when they seem to give up there is a constant fixation with their issue, an almost constant bowing down of their conscious spirit, eyes down, sad, and completely negative about their chances to ever get better. For the most part, a person even though they may present all the abilities to improve their lives, they dwell on their losses, doubting and negative about any chance for improvement.

"Look up, up is always good. Lift your face out of the muck."

Many people believe and often ask the question; "If God is a loving God why does he create the muck I happen to find myself face down in."

"It is because I am a loving God that I created this reality for you to enjoy. As in all creation, in order for it to have substance, it also casts a shadow. The shadow is not darkness but is often used by darkness, because darkness is so afraid of the light, it lurks in the shadows."

"The objects I created are not the shadows, but merely cast

the shadow as they block out the light. The shadow is merely the area created space subject to a reduced or absent light, without physical form, unable to harm you, but it is here that darkness lingers."

"The muck is not the enemy, it is merely being used by the enemy to inflict harm. Look to the light, the darkness flees from the light. Add light to your life and the darkness must flee."

"Back to the rainbows and my promises; I keep all my promises, and I show you all the time and whenever you look in the form of signs, visions, dreams, sounds, recollections, rainbows, rainbow-like appearances of colors on objects, angles in their appearance or directed actions, birds, pets, butterflies, snowflakes, healing, and the list goes on and on into infinity. I basically show myself in every creation for those who are looking."

"Ask and ye shall receive, for you have not because you ask not. Believe that you are loved, and as a loving Father I would hold back no good thing from my child who asks."

I guess this is where so many people fail, especially when it comes to severe injury or diseases, they are so convinced by the world that certain things are just incurable or permanent, that they are not willing to even ask, or asking represents a false hope for a miracle. The majority of the people who walk through the door, while believing miracles do happen, they happen only to others and not to them.

I must say I have been perplexed myself why some people seem to be miraculously healed with what is said to be incurable afflictions. Yet many suffering from the same, also at times ask yet are met with silence or even worsening issues?

"People need healing in many different areas of their life, often unaware or worse ignored by their own hearts, and it is in this area that choices are made whether they chose to believe God or believe what they have been told. It boils down to choice, every soul has free will do as they choose, to listen to what the world has told them or do they listen to God?"

"Health, Wellness, and Real healthcare is engulfed and dependent upon the realization of God-given truths, and the application of these truths, within each of you for the realization of the promised outcomes granted to each by the reality of the entire world I have created for you in this life, this totalitarian soul that encompasses your entire life."

"Jesus my son and the physical manifestation of my own self made physical is the greatest of these promises, He demonstrated to My children the free gift of healing granted each and every one of you. Everyone who was willing to lift their head, or eyes, hear or come, turn towards Me, call, all who were willing to and but for a moment believe, look in the direction of god for resolution for the storms these afflictions cause you, received healing."

"Doing anything with the intention of doing what God would have you do, no matter the situation, storm, or plan, it has within itself that moment's reality, in its creative momentous perspective, subtlety the result to form a real event in the spiritual realm which is more significant than any physical movements these actions may be facilitated in the physical created universe, that is the physical universe of which your bodies are aware and reside. For the created universe is merely a fraction of the whole in comparison to the physical boundaries of entirely of creation, your own scientists have stated and presented this repeatedly."

I know this fact myself and always have found it perplexing the thought of so much space. How infinitely small atoms actually are, or viruses for that matter. The vastness of space between planets or stars, or the spaces that science would tell us resides even between the relatively small actual physical boundaries of the components of atoms is almost unbelievable. There is in the subatomic level much more space than actual energy taking up space. The distances and emptiness being almost inconceivable.

Understanding the complexity and supernatural significance of the order of the universe it makes sense that we must look to the supernatural or how we believe if we even hope in the least to find a solution to an affliction and stimulate healing, in essence, turn on a God gene?

"The physical is a mere fraction of the whole and is a reflection of the spiritual. So as the physical universe is but the smallest portion of the perceived reality, so are your bodies but a fraction of the existence you know as your soul."

PETER J COLLA

Adam Is In Everything

Science will tell us that we are merely a conglomerate of energy; particles of negative charges revolving around positive ones with a few neutral ones thrown in there for good nature. Isn't God wonderful, everything in His creation from the largest to the smallest mimics each other, and ultimately Him, as to place His perfect design on the fingerprints of everything we may take the time to look at, and then hopefully give Him the glory for the creation?

In my own observations positive particles or in this case people with truly positive spirits, those who have a Good God dwelling within, rest in a balance of secure stability knowing where they are, and more importantly where they are going, having a sense of balance in the cosmos. Neutral particles can come in close proximity to the positive ones, close but not quite touching, there is no fear, no repulsion, just calm acceptance with a mutual dance of a subtle rotation. Their relationships, even though seemingly held together with threads of a seemingly insignificant and immeasurable force, this force although seems to be blessed with energies of unfathomable consequence, as though the creator himself placed an enormous amount of importance that these bonds, the same force when split would produce enough power to topple all the creations of men.

But not so with the negative ones that circle at a distance, always in motion, unsure of where they are at any particular time, flying around in multiple looping chaotic ovals that speak more of irregularity and nervousness than anything remotely stable. These small almost inconsequential particles and I say almost, because each while taken on its own merit from a worldly standpoint, seem unimportant, being tiny, easily replaced, and prone to chaotic and irrational behavior. They are constantly jumping around from one place to another in a haphazard exchange of static irritation. The energy exchange of this static irritation is minor on a one to one basis, requiring these little pathetic particles to join forces with many of their cohorts in order to issue any kind of measurable effect. In contrary to their positive brothers, the negative ones must join in an incalculable quantity of others to make an effect that might mimic the power of the positive ones, such as seen in a lightning bolt, even a small discharge from the nucleus has a broader and more permanent effect on its surroundings when splits occur.

And what is further an interesting fact is that the negative particles are repelled by the positive ones, no the negative ones flee from the positive ones because the positive particles remain stationary and its the negative particles that leave. "And darkness looked upon light comprehending it not, darkness fled!"

Let us suppose that these particles are nothing more the composites of electromagnetic oscillations, as science would have us believe, which is the very same kind of energy that makes up the sound. And to further stretch our limit of faith in their suppositions, science would have us believe that these incredibly small particles which relative to their size orbit at incredible distances from each other; It has been supposedly scientifically proven, for example, if a standard proton of a nucleus of an atom was merely the size of a basketball and it sat in Chicago, the closest electron would be the size of a pea and be the distance to Kansas City away. But somehow they are being held together by some immeasurable force, attractions so strong that they can form bonds that are strong as diamonds, making them somehow also impenetrable to a blending of other unwanted visitors, even though these large gaps, these pea-sized so-called insignificant creations.

But the bonds of the positive ones, the likes of which when

mere grams are split, not destroyed, but their initial bond split, form altered, discharge energy of a caliber so magnificent it can take out entire cities of things man built. It was material the size of a penny that fuels atomic bombs. "What God has brought together, let no man bring apart!"

And all of this magnificent power a result of something equivalent to the spoken Word. Wow, if the Bible is merely the writings of men, what genius that these men, for they knew without the aid of modern instrumentation and centuries of learned reference that the universe was "Spoken" into creation. So Moses without the advantage of thousands of years of our so-called evolved intelligence was able to guess that everything was created from the sound when he wrote "God SAID let there be...", and we are supposed to believe this was a random guess on his part not inspired by God Himself, I think not!

Everything that is seen, touched, smelled or tasted, can speak to the glory of God if one will just take the time and look close, even science.

"Infirmities of all types, whether they be sicknesses, injuries or afflictions are the attacks of the moment, momentarily or even those that can last a lifetime, all are attacks from the outside. The awareness of these needs to be placed back on

them to understand them, learn from these experiences and overcome, this is the path to wisdom. To do this you will need to relearn what has been taught and more importantly what is believed about these storms."

Over the course of the next few months, I began to see a distinct change in the way the patients reacted and healed. People would commonly comment about various aspects of the healing process they until recently either didn't witness or just didn't experience because it wasn't there.

God soon taught me about storms in the form of a vision or dream not long after that words came in.

"Let me teach you about the true nature of storms"

"While storms are the attacks perpetrated upon large groups of individuals and areas of My creations, sicknesses and afflictions are the storms that are perpetrated against the individuals singularly and specific for each of you, granting your own momentous opportunities to overcome and continue down the path of the journey I intend in the life I have given you."

"They are like unto hurdles in a race, each an opportunity to jump over and you continue down the path before you."

"Some afflictions, like some storms, like some battles in wars, are physically not able to be overcome, and it is for these individuals and but for Me, the One and Only, resulting decision making Entity, the ultimate finality, the alpha and omega, of creative placement in the garden perspective, a realization of when a spirits time within their given soul needs to leave the human awareness physical so-called reality realm and return to the real and totalitarian primarily spiritual, completely enlightened realm of the heavenly realms, those either and both with Me and away from me, depending upon your own choice as a spirit."

"I would have that every one of you would get out of the boat and come to me, for it is in this moment that you do not calm the storm, it is in this moment of water walking that you do not need to. The storm can not kill you, only doing nothing or looking to the abyss for a solution can."

What Doesn't Kill You Makes You Stronger

"But for those who happen to survive the storms, is granted another promise; What doesn't kill you makes you stronger."

In health care this statement while I have heard it said my entire life seems to be the hardest to comprehend. In some cases, people are born with issues, or later have such dilapitating injuries, illnesses or accidents that seem to never get better or if they survive they seem to suffer, leaving the observer with a perplexing realization that the statement what doesn't kill us makes us stronger just doesn't apply to them?

"But it does, it applies to everyone that survives, what doesn't kill you makes you stronger is not just a statement to boost morale, but an inevitable truth that merely needs to be realized. People survive and become greater in themselves or better, but in many cases delve only on to that which is lost rather than looking at the miracle of healing

and the realization of the gift of getting stronger the survival realizes. This is a truth, and truths are rained down on everyone's heads as indiscriminately as rain upon all the children heads equally and freely, another promise, one and the same! Truths like rain don't have to be accepted to be experienced, but acceptance is the first step in understanding."

"Give me an example of anyone you have treated that you might think didn't get stronger?"

I have personally treated many examples of people who either have lost limbs, gone blind, ruptured disks, or just people who have suffered from sicknesses especially brutal ones such as cancer who while they seem to get a little better, a fraction maybe through relief of pain doesn't seem to get better then they were before but the most dramatic case that comes to mind was when I first started treating the case of JW?

"Tell me what you remember about JW?"

I remember early in my career a man by the name of JW, and while that is not his name, I have no idea how I might find him, if he is still alive to ask him permission to speak about my experience with him, so I will change the name, as I do with every example of real people I write about, to protect their privacy.

One day JW rolled into my office being pushed in his wheelchair. He was severely disfigured, having nearly half of his body ripped off in a heavy construction accident.

As the story goes JW was in charge of manning the end of an enormous digger on the end of a conveyor belt-like machine having multiple digging buckets clawing into the ground as massive amounts of earth were dug away and then displaced along in a conveyor-like manor back behind the larger machine to later be picked up by other large loading machines.

JW expressed that there was a fail-safe at the end of the machine that would override the controller back in the cab of the almost house size machine so that if he was in trouble the machine would immediately shut down. But on many occasions, this shut off would be defective, and because of the great amount of debris and dust kicked in the air it was impossible for the controller up in the cab to see the front man all the time.

In this particular day, as much as he could remember, a large stone was ripped from the ground under where he stood and he fell in with one leg having his boot become caught by the teeth of the large digging claw, dragging him into the machine and ground.

He woke up moments later being rushed to the hospital, died at least five and maybe seven times on the operating table just to finally be saved as finding himself now in this wheelchair for life.

The claw must have pulled down onto his right shoulder because nearly half of his body was gone. His right shoulder, half of his right side of his chest, his whole right hip and below were gone. His left leg was severed halfway across the middle of the thigh, all of these left this poor man disfigured, and with severe scoliosis not able to sit straight in any practical chair.

But that wasn't all, his face was maimed to the point where he had lost half of his jaw, one of his two eyes and literally a part of his face and skull leaving him disfigured to the point where it was amazing he could even be alive.

He told us he wanted to have treatment for the pain, suffering from pain every day and constant. We treated him for a while, and being nearly twenty-five years ago I don't remember much about him or whether or not he got better, I do remember he came in for a while, received a fairly large settlement from the accident, and had the same caregiver come in, always with him.

I do remember being intrigued with the various stories of his multiple times he died, of which he would share them with me in detail. One particular time sharing that he had on each occasion died raised out of his body and looked down at the scene of the operating table, hearing the conversation, even knowing when the doctors would speak about giving up and allowing him to just put out of his misery.

One occasion he spoke about clearly lifting out of the multiple floors of the hospital then to see a man being moved out of a helicopter on the roof. He later told the doctor, even reporting on exactly what the man was wearing and how he had a head wound when arriving.

JW would speak of the light, and the tunnel experience but had very little memory of this and if he did wasn't sharing further details with me.

He is a good example if what doesn't kill you makes you stronger, how could he possibly ever be stronger?

"The part you do not know about JW is the attack right at

the moment of his injury. JW was divorced and had not seen his children for years struggled with the guilt and pain of this separation. On the day of his injury, he was struggling with thoughts of regret and un-forgiveness, un-forgiveness for himself."

"The woman you saw who pushed him into your office was the same woman who cared for him right after his injury, soon fell in love with him and eventually even married him."

"JW was a half of a man before his injury having his wife and children ripped from him, after the injury he became a whole man again, having love and the union of man and wife in his life. He may have had half a physical body, but in his mind and more importantly in his spirit, he was a whole man, much greater then he had ever been before."

"He shared his story with you and dozens of others, inspiring through his suffering, yet testifying to the true healing nature of Me. He used his body now to inspire, challenge, even confront people in their deepest fears, the fragile nature of this life."

"As with JW and others like him whether they are involved in accidents, injuries even of their own misguided steps,

storms brought unto them merely by being in the wrong place at the wrong time, or delivered to them one spoon at a time like baby food from the spoon of a misinformed mother, the results are all the same; if you survive the ordeal, you become stronger, in spirit, mind, and even body?"

Walking Towards The Crevasse

A Dream;

Rolling majestic hills crested with outcroppings of sands and stone, miles of valleys and rivers, green and browns and reds all lines in ordered placement, painted in such a perfect canvas as to leave no doubt as to who is the artist. How grand is the view from the air, no shadows to block your view except perhaps those of the clouds flying just a bit higher and on slightly out of reach? A long way down, how free the feeling of gliding along the airways of height, gently turning, soaring, dipping, and ascending at the very whim of thought.

From this birds-eye-view a person can almost feel the subtle changes in altitude as we sore higher and then dip lower, a bird-like sensation breeze blowing on your skin, the feeling of the air flowing by in an invisible pool of currents and streams, pushing against your skin as the forces of air thrusts hard up in their upward lift, ever wrestling with the forces of gravity that keep our feet firmly on solid ground. Far below small shapes, are those buildings, vehicles, or just some rocks, loose lying materials of all shapes and sizes both useful and discarded, awaiting a future point when they will become useful again?

"Is this how it feels, to be a bird?" the small seven year old boy says to himself, but also out loud, not only in a nonchalant manner, but with such self confidence and absolute assurance that at any moment some invisible companion will just materialize and answer his question without a single break in step.

"I have flown many times in my dreams, and I can't wait for the day when just like my dreams, I will launch off into the air and not worry about the landing back on the ground."

He walks, yet so much more meanders in a nonchalant manner, lending the observer to the conclusion that this small boy is completely and utterly at peace in the endeavor he is engaged upon. He could be anyone in the world, a prince wondering through his kingdom, a content husband dreaming of his beloved wife, a free spirit without care, content and happy, quite different from those that present themselves from day to day alone. Not a care in the world and completely oblivious to the surrounding noises or even so much as the world and all the complexities that are yet to infiltrate into the private bubble of a world that this young lad has captured and made his own.

"Yes, it is, but so much more!", says the strong yet soothing voice, clear and deep, lying within his head and at the same time permeating every part of his soul. The voice is one the young toe-headed boy has heard his whole life, a calming voice, one filled with complete acceptance, in a world of often un-acceptance. Somewhere down deep this young lad knows deep within his chest, in the very heart of his sole that this voice is not his own, it is of another, one greater, one older, one always right, always true, but most important, One always loving.

Complete peace.

"Let me show you, close your eyes and walk, let the feeling of the air flow under your hands listening with the subtle changes of the ground beneath, as you, not your feet pass over."

The boy closes his eyes because as he had so many other times in his life, he completely trusts the voice, knowing instinctively that this voice has only his best interests in heart.

"There is an order of things in the world, you can not always see them, one thing feels like this, but is really that, a good thing might seem good but can be bad for you, and a tough thing, a thing that almost seems unbearable will almost always be a very, very good thing. While you feel alone, you are never alone and not in any way do you ever experience anything that you don't in some way experience something altogether different. When you see it, smell it, taste it, hear it, feel it, that single part of the world, becomes a part of you and your own private world, forever with you, becoming a small piece of who, you are and what you will become forever." "So be careful and choose well."

"What is forever?"

"That is such a good question; what do you see with your eyes closed?"

"Nothing, black, maybe something, shapes sparkles I don't know."

"How high is up, left or right, or even down, can you see the edge?"

"No"

"So is it with me, without end, up and down, left and right, forever!"

A small smile crosses the young boys face as he hears the sweet words caress his lonely heart, and he almost coos in some gentle response, one that no other living soul in the entire universe is aware of except the one who spoke to him, and He not only hears the sweet sound, but feels every emotional inkling, with all the importance, significance, and depth that the very breath indicates. He loves the young boy for it, but oh so much more then a normal love, for the boy is the very essence of that being, He who created the entire universe for him. His dear baby child, His son, His light, He would give it all for, He has, and would have given it all again, if only for him alone, so great is the love of a Father for His son, nothing and no one can keep a Fathers love from His son, if the son but reach up and take it.

This brief interaction, which was, and most likely is; only as brief as a blink of an eye. It was as real and significant as an entire creation, to the one who decides for Himself, what and exactly when anything is important. Yet, the boy moves on oblivious other than just in a very childlike needing way, and as oblivious as the baby is to the source of the milk in the bottle, but ever so thankful for the satisfaction and elimination of the pain within the body when hungry.

Any feeling or awareness the young boy may have felt from this interaction floats by nearly as unaware as the ground passes under. This doesn't stop him, and as he walks for what seems to be forever, eyes closed not slowing for a moment. What initially started with a small sense of apprehension quickly turns into nervous fear laced wonder. All this conversation passed in a blink, between steps, and as the boy realizes he is still walking with his eyes closed, he briefly resists the temptation to open his eyes, even as fear begins to wrap its tentacles around the very fabric of his thoughts.

"Don't worry, I won't let you get hurt, I will always be with you, I have always been with you, and nothing or anything can ever keep me from you, because I love you so much, my

precious sweet child." "Open your eyes now and stop!"

The young boy stops only inches from a crevasse he knew was ahead but was sure it was far to the left of where he was walking, and he had strayed much farther off the normal path then he had ever expected. The crevice was not extremely deep but may have injured him had he fell in unexpectedly.

"Seeing and experiencing the crevasse can have a lasting effect on your soul, depending on first how you experience it and second what you feel about that experience."

PETER J COLLA

Your Soul Is A House

"Your life is the accumulation of everything you experience in your body, mind, and spirit. Your life is your soul. Sicknesses and infirmities are storms affecting your body from the outside in. You decide how you will deal with them."

"Your soul is as of a house, a house with many walls, and chambers, doors, and windows. I build you perfect with clear crystal golden glass walls. The house I build, you form the foundation early in your life, and add to your house good and bad each day with the choices and experiences you live through."

"There are five portals into your soul and that's through your eyes, ears, mouth and nose, and through your skin. It is in and out of these that you chose what to receive and give throughout your lives."

On a quantitative or at least an experiential level there are four ways the insides of our bodies feel, becoming aware of the outside world this is through light, sound, taste/smell, and feeling. The light through our eyes with sight, sound for the most part through our ears with hearing, food or chemicals and various organic through our mouth or nose, and the last are interactions with the outside world through the sensations they stimulate on our skin, joints and the other inner movement receptors of the body.

Science would call these the five senses being sight, hearing, touch, taste, and smell, and even has spoken and become aware of a possible sixth sense, a yet unknown sense or feeling rectors that somehow make us aware when danger is imminent or intuition about one thing or another.

It is also taught in psychology that we have the ability to encapsulate our experiences into rooms allowing us to close off more dramatic or painful experiences of our past into chambers until we are able to properly handle them. Often these chambers represent the most fearful and traumatic areas of a persons' life they choose to lock up and forget.

"This description is not far from the truth except the chambers are made by me and hold the various treasures of the life I give you. All the love you experience, all the joys, the other souls you dance with through the garden of your life are held in treasure chests in the many-chambered mansions of your souls."

"Closing off yourselves to the storms and tribulations in your life is the equivalent of allowing a wild animal into your house and then locking it up in a room rather than dealing with it or chasing it out."

I have seen it often with people, patients who suffer from chronic issues, there is often unresolved issues that surround the injury they are presenting with. People who come with back pain, whether spontaneous as they may seem to occur often find itself manifesting with people who have issues in their life where they have problems with the burdens they are carrying whether it be in their own personal lives or in the workplace.

Understanding the basis of the problem is the first step in preventing the problem from reoccurring, and it is only when they deal with this preemptive initiating factor that they are able to effectively address the issue in a complete and long-lastingly. It is for this reason that the initial evaluation is so important for the proper evaluation of all the injury factors to be assessed.

While this evaluation process, especially determining the complicating or initially preempting factors was stressed earlier in the education of medical providers learning process, over the course of the last ten to fifteen years these interests have been less and less required and even to the point where it is completely ignored stating more of an interest for a single isolation of affected tissue, a specific chemical or particular gene. A sort of caring less for the whole person than just putting a label or single diagnosis code on it and treating the injury as limited and regimented as possible.

"Everything that gets into your house either you let in, bring in or have delivered in through the doors and windows in your house, this includes injuries."

"Sicknesses are spiritual, they manifest using unsuspecting and often unknowing agents that deliver their dark agendas against my children. They knock on the doors, you feel this as pain, discomfort or fear and open the door with your own words when you claim them as your own."

That is so true, when I first was educated almost forty years ago people still believed they "came down with", "were afflicted with", "were suffering from", or "caught" this or that, now they say "I have" this or that, or "I am" a this or that name of an injury. I am a diabetic, an amputee, a heart patient, a cancer patient, an addict, a rheumatic patient, and the list goes on and on.

"You have the power given by me to be and thus become what you claim unto yourselves. Your words have the greatest power in them to affect the universe you know at the moment and forever.

Jesus said; It is not what goes into the temple, but what proceeds out that can make a man corrupt.

"Yes"

PETER J COLLA

A Cork Upon the Ocean

"You are as unto a small cork bobbing upon the waves of the waters of this world, and as well, you are also the essence of the of all the waters of the world residing in every aspect of the whole limitless and infinitely created perfection."

Another example came to mind when thinking about this life as it was created. In 2016 my wife and I considered the position of a person as related to the more mind, body, and spirit therapeutic effectiveness, and how it may find its place in the entire scope of the universe as it was created, it was at this moment an image emerged perhaps it was a dream, or a momentary flash of understanding, that later transcended in the discussion as it birthed its way from thought to spoken word.

The world or science community would like to refer to us as a most insignificant speck on a world spinning on its axis 24,000 miles per hour at the equator. The Earth revolves around the sun at 18.5 Miles/second that is an astonishing 66,600 miles per hour. Our solar system is traveling around our own galaxy at an astonishing rate of 143 miles per second, and our own galaxy while the total seems to change every year based on newly discovered finding and further disproven old theories, the most recent figure seems to be that at any one time our bodies are hurtling through space at an astonishing 1.3 miles per hour.

What is amazing is that if we are to believe that we were created with a purpose and are truly significant then how does that fit in the infinite spectrum of the universe? Perhaps we must reconsider the actual small reality of what science would call our actual physicality.

Let us take a common example of the basketball size atom nucleus of hydrogen, the electron would only be smaller than a ping pong ball and circling almost 2 miles away. Now if we were even a hundred feet in the air that basketball would shrink in perspective from the field of vision to nearly nothing and the ping pong ball would definitely be an invisible speck against the distant background. Science says the space between the atoms even greater and all the space in between completely empty.

All that empty space infinitely small specks against a background of space and nothingness, kind of like outer space and the speckles of pinpoint stars against an infinite background of empty space.

Kind of like a cork floating on the ocean.

So if our life at least the physical being of the energy that represents our body is by example the cork on the ocean, then the waves, wind, sun baking on the surface, the rain, and even fishes nibbling on the cork, represent all of the stimuli our minds have to process. Basically, our mind comprehends the individual waves and every aspect of the wind it feels. All of these being categorically placed on the library shelves of our mind, for later reference to access and compare to new experiences all good or bad.

"The realm of the physical body is as a cork."

Even if the cork eventually is destroyed or ages to the point where it may fall apart and sink, the atoms that make up the cork merely move on to other functional parts of structures found around the relative space occupied by the cork. As parts of the cork move on like hairs on our head fall to the floor, so do the energies of the many atoms and specific everything that takes up any small fraction of space, in the vast continuum we call the physical universe, move to another place in the spectrum of what we understand as this momentary physical space.

Your mind is the experiential recording of everything that happens to the cork.

Science or more over the scientists would say that while energy can change form, it cannot be either created or destroyed and if this so speaks right into the everlasting statement of what God has said to describe the creative universe He has created.

Let us then suppose that our experiential mind or the consciousness of which we experience dwells in the ocean. Then every experience, every thought, every action, or reaction is like dropping a drop of ink into a glass. By the law of diffusion, the ink molecules will disperse to a point of lower concentration until the entire glass is completely blended evenly throughout and will distribute itself evenly throughout the entire volume. What is the limit of this; a bowl, a swimming pool, a lake, an ocean?

So if the spirit our spirit gets their drops of emotions and beliefs deposited by the actions, and reactions of this life then into the ocean is like the place where it is deposited, then what is the expanse or limit of the spirit? The answer;

the entire ocean! The ocean is God, our life expands throughout this realm and becomes a part, seemingly insignificant part, but if the ocean is ever changed even by a single drop, is it not completely significant, because it has the ability to "create change". We are truly created in the image of God.

"Your spirit is the ocean, I am the ocean and everything beyond."

The drops of ink as they spread out throughout the entire unlimited expanse of this ocean, not limited by time, or space, everlasting and infinite. We are not the ocean, for we didn't create it, but we are part of it as we created in its image and thus through an experiential gift we call life we get to add to it good or bad as we chose in the desire of our existence.

Believing is the essence of existing in the realm of the spirit. A person can have something happen to it physically, in one part or fractional place on their body, since it with the complexity of the mind, placing the experience into the vault of calculation of memories past, present and even in the future, but the real experience in totality encompasses the complete effect each and every moment of this life has on the total beliefs of the spirit, what the spirit believes about a thing or event?

If we are truly mostly spiritual beings, and the spirit has the far greatest effect on our lives, then it must also be true for health and healing.

The body is the smallest fraction of you, the now, one moment of one day.

As I was showed the body is the least of the amount of actual physical realism in the created universe only taking up a fraction of the existed space in one moment of time and space. The mind is a databank, in effect a storage library of all past and present stimulus the body receives through the actions and experiences of your life with the outside world, as well as the storage house of every spoken as well as heard word, the every images your eyes receive, and the every taste or reaction the food your body takes in experiences, the very dreams and thoughts you contemplate throughout this short physical life which represents your life.

The mind with its accumulated awareness and even greater recordable unawareness representing past, present, future plans, hopes, and prayers, while the spirit, on the other hand, is infinite.

"Ok, My turn;"

Yes, if your body is a simple as a cork floating on the waters of the ocean, your mind is the accumulation of every aspect of the waves that gently rock aspiringly challenge the strong surface of the cork throughout its existence. The movements, the wetness, the very chemical makeup of the waters splashing against the cork as it bobs up and down and randomly floats across the seas, the infinite feeling of the days' warm sun on its surface each moment's new skin. The cool nights, an exact and methodical record of every bird or fish picking at the surface the cork, even the interactions of all of the other corks as they pass by.

Your spirit is as a great ocean, vast almost limitless and as infinite as the surface of the oceans waters, as deep as the very recesses of the greatest abyss, far beyond the ability to seep its most intricate touch, much higher than the highest climbing water molecule up unto the great currents of glorious winds. Within this air, the waters of your thoughts and dreams dance, the deeds and words you speak in every thought the realities of your every creation.

Each drifting from time to time into the heavens, just to fall back down in their own time, symphonies in the clouds of heaven realms just to cool to droplets or crystallize into solid dreams of created ideas that when touched with good and godly aspects form the most beautiful and individually perfect snowflake formations, fall to earth in real memories.

Tears they drop down the faces of the most perfectly created children any Father could ever hope to realize. Even deeper then you can possibly comprehend in the deepest recesses under the surface and throughout the entire world, throughout every living creature, they touch, flowing constantly transferring their actual physical and molecular essences through the entire created world.

It is as a flowing ballet of created energy amassed into a momentary and everlasting masterpiece of harmonic and perfected landscape formulated for one purpose, to exhibit the grandeur and complexity of the I-Am. And you do it every single moment of every day.

The ocean in essence in God manifested, and you are a part of that creation part of it, not all of it but not lacking any part of it as well.

Sicknesses and injuries are no more than momentary effects on the cork at one moment in time and space, and have very *little effect if any on the entire ocean, as a matter of fact, the actual events of a particularly aggressive wave or irritating fish have only the most fractional effect on the ocean as a whole.*

When dealing with sicknesses if you will address your treatment or how you TREAT these attacks relative to their significance compared to you, you will have the greatest chance of overcoming, in fact, you will be guaranteed to overcome because it is promised."

If the body is the least of you, the mind more, and the spirit the greatest, then the treatment should reflect this. But in the world, as it stands in health care today the opposite is true. You can share the wisdom I shared with you regarding insurance and spiritual enslavement.

PETER J COLLA

Problem with Healthcare Today

"Healthcare is a temple"

"The lives of the children you treat, in your present medical system, you merely guide them in paths that are directed and ever increasingly controlled by entities that have one desire; to steal My children's souls."

Let me describe in the next few paragraphs the part of the story the media refuses to bring to our attention, even though they are quite knowledgeable about it themselves. I am aware of this information because I have wallowed in it for nearly thirty years, myself being a medical provider with my own private physical therapy practice, as well as working through various specialties within this field for this entire time. I have witnessed the degradation of a profession, of a calling, of an industry, almost as it has unfolded in front of me, like watching a piece of fruit whither, rot, and eventually decay right in front of my eyes, all the while also seeing the attempts of the media to place the blame where it shouldn't have even been.

Let us find a villain we can point the finger of accusation at, and granted a small fraction of truth can be shown, towards the Doctor's, but most importantly away from the true culprits; the insurance and pharmaceutical companies.

It astonishes me how many people have been duped or are being blindfolded to the corruption, either way, most people have no idea of the truth regarding how little the insurance companies really care for them. No, the truth is, they care for only one thing, taking total control of the people, and getting paid for it in the process. Stealing from God those first-fruits, those gifts of our labors, He intends so desperately for us to use for His kingdom, as blessings for our lives, our children, each other, expressions of love, instead of given to a greedy spirit who only wants to invoke fear to steal from God, while control and enslave His children.

Medical Insurance really did not become a term of common knowledge even in the insurance agencies themselves until the second half of the twentieth century, finding its foundation on the heels of accident insurance. This following a series of dangerous endeavors that seemed to injure or kill many people. These events while sensationalized and basically used by the media, early life insurance companies would capitalize on this new media driven fear in order to make people became scared by earlier tragic events, such as the Titanic, into purchasing insurance in order to purchase some kind of "assurance" against a future accident might occur.

Soon the insurance companies saw the huge profits that could be generated by receiving small premiums, especially after they played and even feed on these fears, but of course, there were still just so many of these tragedies, it only affected a small portion of the public.

It is was about this same time a huge media propaganda campaign was initiated to basically scare the public into the need to stop trusting in God for their health security, but rather an entity that has through lofty promises itself boldly attempted to provide security even in the event of the most tragic and fear-driven event; death. So maybe innocently at first, or perhaps by design, the life insurance companies tried to usurp for almost one hundred years the security only God can give, the security over death. When this seemed to work, why not try it with other areas; fire, transportation or auto, home security, mortgage, renting, business, loans, and eventual heath itself?

In essence, take the place of God give assurances that everything will be alright.

It is first important to realize that these same families also control the banks, oil, federal reserve, weapons manufacturing, who are the major stockholders in all of the fortune five hundred companies, including the media, and pretty much lust to control everything and every creation under the sun, that same creation of which God had originally intended for us, every one of us, also started the major insurance companies, or have retained at least a controlling interest in every one of them, worldwide.

It was not long after insurance companies started providing comprehensive medical insurance, as a matter of fact only a very short time, by the early eighties, that these same insurance companies began a campaign to acquire ownership in hospitals, and within a couple of years, by only 1983 had already purchased 20% of the hospitals in the United States, and today own almost 90% of them. Why?

This brilliant move grants two very important components for success, and guarantees expansion of the control of the medical insurance industry. Let me explain;

Now lets say you are a greedy old man who owns an insurance company, or worse yet a dark spirit whispering in his ear, and you know the goal is to make enormous amounts of money at the expense of the general public; problem is, if your company is a public traded company, (and why wouldn't you want it to be public and generate a profit, you want to control the markets as well), there becomes a need to not show to much profit! First and foremost, for the justification of increasing premiums and reducing payable services can only be believed by the public, if a hardship is demonstrated, stating a necessity to raise rates must be made. But more importantly, is the absolute must, to make certain the peasants don't grab pitchforks and look for a public burning, after realizing the vast amounts of Gods blessings that have all been stolen from the mouths of our children!

So where to hide those enormous bundles of stolen gold? Answer; buy the people who they pay the most money to, then pay it to them, thus themselves! As of today, insurance companies or at least the subsidiaries thereof, own almost "all" of the major hospital's in the US, and are presently attempting to acquire the larger firms of general practitioners (Doctors), as well as specialist, and if not the insurance companies, then the pharmaceuticals. But we should not forget who owns the major pharmaceutical companies as well, yes the same people who own the banks and insurance companies!

So the greedy old man concocts this brilliant plan; buy up the hospital's, drive the bills up so high the public becomes scared of absolute ruination if they find themselves within the grasp, or the need to send their children into such a place for life-saving care. Funnel huge portion's of insurance premium sums of money to them, paying without question ridiculous fees such $250.00 for the little plastic bucket, or a one and half inch tube of toothpaste, the same products you can buy at "The Dollar Store" for much less than a dollar. Show fewer profits on the insurance companies book's, and what a bonus, "we can blame the rising cost of insurance premiums on rising health care fees charged by the Doctors, and the stupid peasants will only have to look at their own medical bill's to see the enormous cost."

Blame the individual Doctor; "see he is rich, it must be his fault!"

Is it such a coincidence that about the same time the insurance companies began to obtain the hospitals, that the rates of the hospitals and all the care surrounding surgeries went through the roof; the early to mid-eighties!

The greatest fringe benefit of this is the scare factor; people seeing the enormous cost's of a typical hospital stay or heaven forbid an operation, become so scared they hardly dare live without insurance. Fear, a powerful weapon to bring the populous under servitude, bring them to their knees, and convince them to give their money, even before it gets into their hands, first fruits, their sacrifice that is brought to the altar of the "one who gives assurance" the insurance company, instead of being used for the children of God, or His kingdom as intended.

Ok, people, I will say this one time!

I have been practicing medicine for twenty-five years in my own practice, but the amount I get paid from health insurance, regardless of what I charge, has not gone up a cent! They, the insurance companies keep us, providers, settling for these frozen rates year in and year out because of contracts; HMO's, PPO's, Industrial Insurance, and the like, and if we have a desire to renegotiate the rate, their answer always is; "if you don't want the contract, the guy down the street will take our clients."

You see my dear brothers and sisters, insurance companies could not care less how many providers or contracting doctors they have, as a matter of fact, the fewer the better. More waiting time for our appointments means less billed visits totally or the ultimate home run; the poor soul just gives up out of frustration when the clinic tells them there is a one-month waiting list. These dark spirits love working with large companies, because the large company does exactly what the insurance company says, and reimbursed the small contracted rates, never daring to irritate the great master with a request to give the poor patient actually what they might need, or what they believed they were paying for when they purchased the insurance policy in the first place. But just shut up and do as they are told. The risk of losing the contract is too big.

Oh sure, there are groups out there that provide a service that is so rare, so new, that if the insurance companies didn't contract, (at least when they don't get away with calling it pioneering, or unproven, and denying it as experimental), there is the public threat of outrage is always what lingers in the back of their minds, so in these few rare cases they have to pay larger fees or are not be able to negotiate reductions.

These doctor's or procedures are rare, usually, specialist surgeon's, new groundbreakers of one or more odd procedure, some new apparatus or medical treatment that very few do or can get their hands on. These are the only ones who usually become the few sequestering the highest paid and annually increasing payout's, but for the most part insurance companies will strive to bring all entities and providers under contract submission, until such time that they have the market covered, it is only then that they can put the actual squeeze on.

And until that day actually takes place, the day they can control all aspects of our health, they will blame the rising cost of healthcare on the Doctors sighting the very few who might get full rates. Little does this poor surgeon know, but for his few years of walking on the top of the payout food chain, he is vilified by the big corporate owned media, and pretty well blamed for all the financial woes of an entire industry.

In Jesus's time tax collector's where used much in the same way, also given a "pittance", and basically made the enemy of the people, to take the true eye off the real villain, the one stealing the money in the first place; the Roman Emperor!

"A system which treats only the body, vaguely or even disregards the mind completely, and does nothing for the spirit or the way you believe, except present ideas of doubt, doom or inevitable destruction has only the least amount of chance for success, and if anything leads more to dependency, addiction and individual enslavement then leading a person to be healed or cured of anything."

So you are saying that all those years of treatment I was only hurting people rather than helping them?

"While your intentions may have been good most of the time, you like others that have fallen into the trap of the system merely to become pawns of that system where greed dictates your choices for how much actual care you will provide, and the underlying drive that presses you forward in your planning and ambitions are a full waiting room or the twenty pieces of silver you receive."

"As long as you participate in their system, you in effect become priests and priestesses in a temple of its dark design. The system as you know it has become and is a temple."

"Truths like promises, like all good things I give all my children in My garden, like the rain, like the snowflakes that fall on receptive faces, each of these perfect flakes gently caress your cheeks in its cool but tender refreshing touches."

"The Wisdom of God is like unto rains that fall down on freely on everybody's head regardless of their position in the garden."

Too many people are deceived in their own self, thoughts of wealth or lack thereof, ridiculous notions of race, nationality, or the many lies are spoken that mislead them into their false fanatical religious perspectives.

"Each of you to hide your heads from the rain, your own outrage often emanating in your voices as you seemingly bury your head in the sand, is not unlike a turtle digging deep within a hole, leaving his vulnerable backside sticking out for attack."

"Turn not away, because such behavior can cause each of you to miss out on the rain freely given and granted everyone who might but look for it."

The Body Alone

How do medical practitioners consider the body, mind, and spirit all at the same time? As a Therapist I have always been taught to consider the most basic point of the injury, trying to identify the exact location an injury manifests, then apply the therapeutic treatment to the specific structures that need to be repaired.

Many people believe the soul to be the small consciousness that rests somewhere in the middle of their chest, softly and inconsequentially pulling them one way or the other, something that is often ignored and often debated by more modern philosophical teachers as to whether it actually exists or not. Modern medicine education teaches us as practitioners to examine and consider, ever increasingly, the most basic physical aspects of the body as we endeavor to treat people.

There has been an increase of anatomization as well as cataloging of individuals into regiments of treatment models and dehumanizing diagnosis codes, ever striving to refine everybody's afflictions into the most simple and routine treatment regiment, at least from an educational and authorization standpoint. This has certainly found itself, at least lately, in an ever-increasing area of medical controlled authorizing of care. People usually don't find this out until they fall knee deep into the world of needing healthcare for themselves or a love-one.

Individual needs and deviation from standards of care take little into consideration as to the specific and variation of individuals, whereby there has been an increased desire by the insurance companies to have a label, again diagnosis code, or name placed on everybody, and thus plug in the corresponding recommended treatment regiment for simplicity and authorization purposes. This has, for the most part, turned medicine into a sort of fast food drive-through window.

"The flaw in this approach to treating, regardless of the affliction, is it leaves the practitioner and patient in a position of chasing the symptoms of injuries and not the injuries themselves."

If a person merely treats the sprain location on the body that occurs when an individual falls, without examining the cause of the fall, then no opportunity develops for the injured person to learn from their fall can be accomplished, the now recovered individual goes back to the lifestyle that caused them to fall in the first place, a time bomb waiting for the next possibly more severe fall to occur.

"Always examine the cause!"

It is my experience, not as much with specific physical injuries, but especially with sicknesses, that often a person is not aware of the specific cause. The exact moment an injury may have started is often vague or in many cases completely unknown.

"If you are willing to believe that every person is ocean size spirit compared to a cork size body floating on the waves, then consider the fact that sicknesses and injuries have large spiritual footprints and only the smallest of actual physical effects on the body. And thus your ability to affect them in the area of healing has the greatest effect when directed in the spirit as only compared to the body."

"Like all attacking agents, they have commonalities that for the persons who are looking are unavoidable." "Remember these are the smallest most insignificant members of the spiritual world, they cannot create they merely desire to wreak havoc, be seen, be feared, and accomplish what they were sent to do."

"They cannot create, so they must rely on the strategies and images they have witnessed in the past."

You have not because you ask not, you see not because you refuse to look, you hear not because you turn a deaf ear towards the truth.

So you are saying that all people have to do is ask and it will be made known to them what is the reason or spiritual significance of any injury or affliction?

"Absolutely, did I not say, if you ask, I will show you, but you must first ask, look or at least be willing to hear."

"*Before Jesus healed anyone the people looked at him, towards him, called to him, began to listen to him, reached for him, even pleaded to him for help for themselves or others they loved.*"

"*They didn't know who he was, some may have sensed it deep down inside, but many merely heard others speaking in astonishment as He passed by, calling in hope; Jesus, Son of David have mercy on me?*"

"*A child that looks towards the light is the first single step in any healing.*"

Warriors, Come Out And Play

"And Jesus asked him saying, what is thy name? And he said Legion; because many devils were entered into him." Mark 5:9

Accident or example, why this particular possessed man did Jesus ask? It is clearly documented that Jesus cast out demons in many people. Even the Pharisees admitted it with their own accusations when they accused Him of casting out demons in the name of demons, as in Matthew 12:24.

But why was this particular man commented on, noted and described, not only in one but two Gospels? Was it perhaps to teach? God doesn't just teach with a single action, but with His entire creation, enveloped in every documented event, there is teaching within teaching, within teaching, within an entire philosophy. Is that not so God? Where can we not look in His entire creation, and ever finding more examples of His beautiful creation, evidence of teaching, as we peel back the layers, like a majestic onion?

No, the demon just didn't give a single name or even many, Jesus knew this, He wanted the demon to reveal important information about the structure and even the makeup of our enemy. He solicited out all the information He wanted to be known, like interrogating a filthy spy, He got everything with a single question.

The demon responded "Legion". Not braggingly, almost as if he had the information was ripped from its mouth. "How silly," our Lord must have thought, when He considered these creatures that tormented His children. How foolish their plans must appear to Him. What did they think, send an entire legion into this poor soul and perhaps make Jesus seem foolish trying in vain to exorcize them?

Of course, He knew their names, He recognized their foul stench coming down the path a mile away. He created them, He knew them very well, but we didn't!

In that one statement the devil's man gave more information away out of its own mouth, they might have been needed to be revealed by Jesus Himself. Why would Jesus even have to dirty His own mouth by explaining the structure and attack mode of the enemy, when He could have one of the devil's own spill the beans for Him.

Oh, it must have been one angry devil that night, and probably a reckoning paid when the devil found out how one of his underlings spilled the beans with its big mouth.

Anybody remotely interested in learning about the structure or makeup of the enemy merely has to examine the word Legion, and the picture that word paints; organization, rank, a particular form of attack, strategies associated with it, weapons used, the training and intelligence the participants held, along with the strengths and weaknesses presented with such a military type organization, all find their way to the canvas layer by layer, brushstroke by masterful brushstroke?

Let us examine for a moment just the structure.

The Roman Army was a highly organized very structured ranking of a soldier all methodically grouped for the purpose of following the instructions and eventual wishes of the supreme commander, usually the emperor. A ruthless horde that was bent on one goal, to bring under servitude all people who stood before their supreme leader.

The smallest group of soldiers eight or so, consisting of the least trained, lowest ranked individuals was called a "Contubernium" and could be perhaps compared to a small platoon. Ten of these small groups would be banded together, this larger collection was called a "Century," because it held approximately 100 men, when you counted the support troops and standard bearer. These men fell under the leadership of one officer a "Centurion, or a captain.

Six Centuries together formed a "Cohort," then ten cohorts would be combined to form a "Legion," the basic military unit! This great group of approximately 6,000 men, and was all under the command of few Tribunes, high ranking officials, perhaps like majors, one or two Prefects, or a single Legatus, all under a General, the Proconsul and eventually the Emperor.

The army was typically deployed in a three tear linear system of structure attack. The first group, "The first in!", where called the "Miles," these were fatigue workers, they had other names but most significant was "Gregorius," which translated; Herd Animal. Represented by the least trained, most disposable, and least effective individuals.

The second tear was composed of greater skilled, better-trained soldiers, these soldiers, received greater equipment, support, the backing of the army itself, power.

The third group was reserved for the veterans, those with the greatest experience, fighting skill, strength, ability to problem solve, these men were highly favored by the commanding officers, they were the ones that received any spoils of the battle if a spoil was received, but with great reward came great responsibility. If a battle was lost often the blame was placed on these, they were the example made, it was their fault. Of course, the leadership would never take responsibility!

We can learn an enormous amount of information by studying the enemy. The supernatural is always represented in the natural. If we are going to battle the enemy, we should strive to understand him, and one way to do this is to understand the structure of their deployment.

First of all the enemies ranks are divided into organized groups, of which the smallest is deployed into small groups of likewise educated, trained, and ill-equipped entities. These, which are considered almost live-stock like, don't think for themselves, only react, they are stupid and prone to making dumb mistakes, they have explosive tempers and at any sign or feel of fear, will go running.

As with the Roman army, and even as seen in the natural, the creatures that have the least abilities, also possess the least intelligence, they have the least adaptive skills, and must join forces with large numbers to have an effect on greater skilled opponents. They attack in groups, so unless their numbers are great, they will only pester and never attack. Herd animals!

I would equate these with demonic irritations, the kinds that attach themselves on a host or in a particular area, and pester, tempt, oppress, or sicken. These are the kinds that inflict chronic pain or irritation to individuals, maybe even addictions, these are the stupid little ones that do nothing but follow you around and nibble on your ankle all day long. These are the ankle biters!

Spot these cowards, and they are likely to take off merely because of being spotted. Just speaking out loud that you are aware of their mischievous dark nature, may be enough for them to go running for the hills. It probably wouldn't hurt to command after them, as they are running; "Don't come back, I'll line all of you and your buddies and give you a real Jesus beating!"

"In this example germs would be the inadvertent creatures being used by the sickness, the sickness is a spirit driving the germs to attack, the spirit uses the many small creatures, physical objects or even people to do their destructive tasks for them, in effect they afflict their hosts then wreak havoc on the target of their attack."

"Understanding the enemy is the great first step in a plan to defeating it."

"Sicknesses are the simplest among the spiritual creation. As in the world with various levels of living creatures from the horse to the simple bacteria, so in the spirit are various

levels of functioning spirits from the greatest angels to the simplest small and weakest."

"When a third of the angels were deceived and fell this group consisted of all variations of spiritual beings, all now choosing dark, not unlike a random selection of one-third of all living creatures on and in the earth."

"As all living creatures of the world were created and placed under the servitude of man, all spiritual creatures were placed under the servitude of the Father."

"Many fell."

People seem to have been programmed or at the very least deceived into believing that sickness and even life-threatening occurrences are somehow like random lurking creatures, some kind of dark beast just outside the limit of their perception waiting to pounce on the unexpected innocents when their guard is down, out of their control, and undetectable yet all-powerful, something to be feared. Words like diseases or syndrome lurking just outside our awareness to sense waiting to pounce on unsuspecting and innocent bodies table to defend themselves let alone cope with the onslaught.

In some cases flaws like genetic predetermined time bombs sit within each of us that like these ticking time bombs are just waiting to have their own undetectable fuses lit, resulting in the unstoppable and irreversible explosion that destroys bodies, lessen life, and create an environment in which the very soul of our existence seems to be feared or even regretted.

"The truth of the matter is actually closer to the model taught then one might imagine, the lie is the ties these sicknesses found woven in the tapestry of your destiny that is in question."

"Sickness and all forms of Infirmity for that matter are merely small insignificant creatures lurking just outside the limits of your perception, but this is not because it is an inconceivably small creature such as a virus or bacteria lurking ready to attack without mercy, or destined by its shear strength of numbers to eventually overcome, it is merely the event of direct impact followed by the individual

decision of being that this attack has been successful in its attempt to distract us from what God truly had in store for each of us."

"Sicknesses and Infirmities are never your destiny but merely unresolved storms you chose to endure rather than overcome. Sicknesses and infirmities are the results of spiritual influences on the simplest of creation. Therein rests one of the first lies; if I created each and every one of you perfect then how could I then create you with flaws?"

I have witnessed many times in the course of years of treating hundreds if not thousands of individuals, an occasional situation where the available resources granted us within our own bodies seems to rapidly and dramatically reduce to the point where mere daily life almost becomes a difficult and almost hopeless endeavor. Nowhere is this seen in what appears as a tragedy as when it appears in the life and final days of a chronically and terminally ill child, and leads many who stand just outside the direct influence of this traffic picture wondering on the purpose, if not the Godliness of such an experience.

Many people are born with flaws not everyone is born perfect, children all the time are born with deformities, issues, syndromes or even sever sicknesses that lead to very untimely deaths and short lives, I have treated many of these. I have witnessed people who have such poverty or on the receiving end of abuse that the thought of some fair shake in this life seems like a joke to them. Are you telling me they have been created perfectly?

"Being born with greater challenges either physically or mentally has nothing to do with flaws, every living person has a purpose a journey to fulfill in the exact place or time I have placed them to experience it." "It is, for this reason, I can say, I have given them everything they need to overcome."

"Tell me what you remember of Justin?"

PETER J COLLA

Justin

Early in my career, I had a patient named Justin, it was a time when I had just started my career and was supplementing my new practice by also doing some work for the local high school district. Justin was a young boy who had an advanced form of Muscular Dystrophy.

For those who don't know this sickness or have ever seen its symptoms play out on a child, basically the child systematically loses the ability to use their arms and legs, basically, the sickness attacks the muscles or in this case the person's ability to control the muscles. These children become increasingly weak, even the most rudimentary activities are extremely difficult. Most of them, by the time they get to high school, are sentenced to a life bound to the wheelchair, many have such limited hand and arm movement they can hardly control the electronic controller of their own chair.

The children have a particular posture that is typical for them they sit straight up in a chair with the exception of the head movements have very little ability to move at all. Justin had all of this, having to sit straight up in his chair, he wore a very restricting back and body brace that held him straight.

It is believed that sitting up straight actually aid them as a means to help or ease breathing or other organic functions usually aided by muscles, the idea is to use gravity to help as much as possible. The result is often these kids receive a very painful and permanent rod in the spine to at least to allow them to sit up without falling over into themselves.

What do I remember about Justin?

I remember remarkably much about him, I remember how there was very little I could do with him, his paralysis was almost complete. No spasm or contracture to speak of, and when I tried to exercise his hands of legs, it was more of a bother to him than a help. The arm or leg would just move with little or no effort, as a matter of fact, he seemed to enjoy more than anything to just play games.

They had a pool table and one of his favorite activities was strapping a pool stick to his arm, and he would after being lined up for the shot, propel his chair forward to hit the ball.

Another activity he seemed to like was playing "super soccer" we would call it. On occasion, we would have access to the gym and with the help from a few student aids we would play soccer with a large exercise ball, this basically amounted to the kids being pushed around in their chairs and hit the ball back and forth sometimes into the goal. They all seemed to laugh with such enthusiasm at any moment their chair would hit the ball. Justin seemed to laugh and get the most excited, often he would insist on driving his own chair, not wishing to be pushed, this would put him at a distinct disadvantage against the kids being pushed by health strong students, but it just didn't seem to bother Justin.

While many of the other children of the class had issues coupled also with severe learning disabilities, often originating from some kind of brain trauma on or around birth, or worse damage caused by alcohol syndrome, leaving children underdeveloped and barely functional from birth with mental abilities barely above that of a newborn for life.

Justin, on the other hand, had all of the normal mental capacities of his normal classmates, which basically meant he had all the desire and feelings as any other child, I guess this made it difficult for me to understand his need to be in special education. But I later learned that he often missed school because of his health and this was the only class, at least at that time where he could receive the one on one attention he needed.

Above everything else, I remember most the fact that with my every waking memory of Justin, he always had a smile on his face. I don't think I ever knew anyone in my entire adult life who seemed to smile all the time like him.

Yet as I bring him back to memory, another thing I do specifically remember about Justin is that one day I came into work and had a discussion with him asking him specifically why he seems to smile all the time?

He casually said; "Because I am so happy, I have everything I have ever wanted, friends, people who I love, who love me, every day seems like a new Christmas present and I love seeing the present unfold."

I remember clearly thinking; how could this boy not be sad seeing other kids run around, go to dances, drive cars, live and do things he knew he would never experience? But all I could muster was a single question; "Do you ever long for the things you can't seem to do; football, swimming, flying a plane, a girlfriend?"

He just looked at me with the sweetest most content smile and said; "I have so many friends, many of the girls, they are all my girlfriends, and as for flying a plane, I fly almost every night in my dreams."

That was one of the last times I ever saw or spoke to Justin, he was out again with what appeared to be some recurring illness, but about a week later I found out he had passed away in the night. It turned out that he had pneumonia, and was unable to cough, his parent put him to sleep and he drowned.

"It's a little tough to see the overcoming possibility, let alone the perfection there?" "I remember he believed in God, even spoke of God freely and beautifully on many occasions. Why could he not be healed?"

"Justin was perfect and overcame, and now you can see as you recall that conversation you had with him only shortly before he died when you asked him why he smiles all the time? He said; because he is so happy."

"Justin was the kind of person who was happy just to be alive and expressed it freely giving back to everyone around him every moment of his life. He in his short life was a true teacher of the gift of happiness.

While others are worried about what they don't have, or should have, or could have, Justin, is just content with everything he did have."

"It was Justine's purpose in this life to show so many other people, yourself included, that happiness is not measured onto people based on what they have, but it is a measure of a persons ability to recognize every gift they have been given them in this life."

"He was healed, and whole, fulfilling everything I would have him experience and give in his life."

"Justin overcame adversity with faith, love, and hope, and now he flies."

The Hole

The Vision of the Hole in the road;

"If one could see disease as it might present itself, one might look at the affliction as if it is a small hole in the road. It is then you the traveler coming along this path, in this new day and a single moment of time, unaware of the hole lurking within a few steps on the path you have chosen, inadvertently gets ready to fall in."

"Some travelers are brought down this particular path by their own choices, some are led by their parents, some are guided as an opportunity to get to a greater place, some are exactly where they were supposed to be, but regardless of the circumstances of the particular path choice, the fact of the matter is the hole awaits."

"Now why does the hole exist? The hole may have been created by the careless actions of those before you, it may have been a natural occurrence in the balance of life around you, it may have been a product of your own hands years before unknowingly, and it may be a trap?"

Now in this case what is exactly the hole, when inadvertently stepped into, possibly causing injury; is the hole the injury, or is it merely the mechanisms used to inflict injury?

When many different persons step along the same path and come to the same hole many fall to the same fate, they step in without noticing it, stumble and even perhaps break their ankle or leg from the fall.

Some overcome the fall by catching themselves with the strength and skill usually granted them by training or youth, some are even given the natural gifts to overcome physically of such tests immediately, some fall but their bodies are strong enough or flexible enough to absorb the blow.

Some are carefully watching enough their steps to avoid the small places where the dangers lie, and some can jump over when the obstacle appears.

"So is the hole the injury?"

"If so why did the hole not hurt the one who jumped over?"

"No, the hole is not the sickness, it was merely being used by the spirit of injury as a mechanism to inflict its task, like a wolf waiting in the hole for an unsuspecting traveler to

venture by. An angry but little wolf, hiding in the recesses of holes that have been deposited in the path of My unknowing little path walkers."

Of course, the smaller, the less experienced, or the more feeble the people, the elderly, or people who have fallen many times before, the more susceptible they are to injuries, the easier prey for the wolf.

The little wolf is injury and is a coward, he hides in the recesses of the dark place, waiting and hoping to sink his hungry teeth into the Godly gift, of the leg, or more vulnerable body part that may present itself.

One may ask why does God allow the hole to exist, but I think we all know this answer, holes in the road are a product of us not taking care of the gifts God has already given us, misuse, or even sabotage by others intent of setting traps or hoping for another to fall.

"No, the hole is not the problem, the little creature, the little nuisance, a little bug for some, with aspirations of being a fierce wolf to others, he is the problem."

"The Hole is not Everything"

If God has been true to his Word, and He always is, then we should merely have to look to our surroundings for the solution to our issue, be it the hole or the pesky little wolf bite.

The hole should be easy, use everything given to us in the immediate hand to overcome the obstacle at hand whether it be among our own God-given gifts; strong legs, quick healthy reflexes, sharp reasoning, or sharp clear eyes, or even material that is within accessibility to overcome the obstacle.

Sometimes even a good strong voice to scare away such a pest, so we can just climb down and try to crawl through the hole, doesn't seem like the most sensible course of action, but how many of us sometimes foolish acting kids seem to choose the most dangerous and impracticable course of action over and over again, instead of just walking around. Then we wonder why we just keep getting a bit over and over again?

"Only Chose Good"

Ok, so the fall into the hole represents the injury, what then? What do you do after the fall, the event, the poor traveler steps into the hole and gets bit.

"Turn on the light, chase away the wolf, and clean up the mess of the storm. The cleaning is the treatment after the affliction."

"As you may have noticed Jesus always followed up every healing with some kind of action; pick up hour mat and walk, go wash in the Jordan, report to the teachers of the temple, go..."

"This is real therapy."

"You must treat in the same perspectives and directions that you were created, if you want good or godly results, you must use good and godly instruments."

"If you want good and godly results you must move in a good and godly direction."

"If you want good and godly results you speak and hear only good and godly words, sounds, perspectives, and plans."

"And if you want a good and godly result you must bath your eyes with light and images that feed your soul with the warmth and love of this good and godly creation. "

That seems like a lot of things a person must do and extremely limiting regarding the world as a whole when it comes to trying to limit what direction you go or what instruments you might use along the way, but even the very sights and sound, even your very words along the way.

"It always boils down to one simple fact; free will. You always have the simple choice to choose in every aspect around you, in this case, whether or not you wish to heal?"

Firemen and Water

"My healing could be described as simply as an image of a Fireman and a Hose."

"When a fire starts in a home, a destructive event or small spark of a flame has occurred which in itself can ignite a chain of events that can destroy an entire house.

"It is no different in the houses you call your souls, of which fires often start by your own hand, by the paths you walk or are taken down, events in and out of your control, hatreds, even unhealthy thoughts, all being brought into your life one spoon at a time. These flammables can then be sparked at the onset of a storm irrupting into a blaze of virtually uncontrollable destruction."

"Wise firemen are called and they first direct efforts to help anyone they can out of the blaze. The next immediate action is to douse the blaze with water, drowning the fire, in essence suffocating the destructive nature of the flame with

life-giving waters, and ultimately hoping to contain the destruction, and ultimately save the house."

"If we attempt to analyze this fire as a parable, and compare it to the sickness process, are the firemen in your opinion the healers?" One might assume so because, without their learned skills and practical application of firefighting, the blaze would have certainly destroyed the entire structure, and possibly killed the innocent inhabitants.

"But no, the firemen do not put out the fire, any more then the fire hoses do, they are merely instruments of the wisdom of the actual gift which is the water."

"Without the water, you could have a thousand firemen standing there waving hoses at the blaze and nothing would happen."

"When men try to heal without giving acknowledgment to Him who healing comes or at least seek the source of that knowledge, it is like a fireman going to a fire without a water source."

So the fire is not the disease either. The fire is merely the resulting symptoms or byproducts coming from the accumulation of flammable or vulnerable materials in the vicinity of the spark and the resulting damaged caused by the small spark.

"As you walk down the paths of your soul, you bring in all sorts of energies into your houses through the many doors and windows of your crystal clear golden glass walls of your mansion. These are the treasures you either pass on to other or hold onto for your selves."

"For those who chose to look only onto light and love and godliness these energetic treasures are drenched in the waters of everlasting health and life. But for those who chose the shadows these treasures you choose to gather are embedded in death and the dark oils that burn hot when sparked into destruction."

In the therapeutic process if we wish to effectively fight the process first we must increase as many water infused energies we can into our houses, but if a fire does occur we must drown it with water?

"The spark is the disease, small, almost insignificant and nothing more than a momentous event in a single fraction of time, like a shot of the gun that starts the race! At the very earliest moment, an attack occurs that is the moment of the greatest effectiveness. And yes, the less accumulated flammables you have the less likely a fire will irrupt when the little flame occurs."

"Water is the true blessing in every form, in every possible process, in every solution."

"I am the Water of Life." "I AM"

Water seems to be the essence of everything that is good, natural or perfect when examining the health and wellness relating to people. The deeper I seem to investigate into various ways to apply treatment the more apparent the use of water become instrumental in this process.

Even earliest in my career, I recall one of the best Doctors I had ever had the pleasure of knowing Dr. Michael Altamura, the true embodiment of goodness in a doctor, a real classic family doctor, the picture perfect country doctor in all of this images love and care. A man I would often see spend his lunch at his desk calling the patients he saw the day before just to find out how they were doing after coming in. He really cared about his people.

One day I presented myself to him with some cut or abrasion and he cleaned the wound with water, told me to let it have some fresh air and light and only bandage it when I thought I might expose it to contaminants. I remember asking should I not use alcohol or other germ-killing washes that I had myself been taught to use? He merely smiled and said; "Alcohol kills cells, and many of those chemical they would have you put on a wound do the same, water is the best cleaning agent in the world and the best thing for washing away germs."

In the natural so is it always demonstrated, as it is in the supernatural.

"Rivers of Life" so did Jesus speak of Himself, the Message, the Word, as He spoke of spreading the good news through the people.

His first miracle as reported by His followers was the turning of water into wine. He took something common, something essential, and converted it into something valuable, pleasurable, something to be consumed, something red.

As it was in the beginning so must it be at the end, one of the last events He also performed was using the wine to symbolize His blood. The wine was involved in His first miracle and at the end as in the final supper, wine plays an intricate role. Wine the representation of His blood. He said specifically; "When You drink, think of me."

Blood is almost completely made up of water, as so is wine, but not quite pure. It has an essence of other things mixed in that make the blood what it needs to be in order for it to give life. A small amount of hemoglobin which is a fascinatingly complex molecule, a carbon-based structure with key points of Iron, this molecule has an enormous capacity to bind with oxygen and delivers life. It is all the other things in the water that give it the ability to perform the various duties we need, or is this perhaps not quite so?

Water has a greater function in the kingdom then I believe we can ever comprehend. Water is used for cleansing, not only the body but also the entire world as in the flood. Water is necessary for almost every vital function in our body. Our body is almost entirely composed of water, and when all water is eliminated as in cremation only a small amount of substance is actually left. We will die of lack of water long before we die of lack of anything else. Water seems to be the key element of life.

Science would tell us that we all come from the oceans, and thus from water, but I believe this world is merely a representation of our body and as we are primarily made up of water, the majority of the earth's surface is also either covered with or retains in it water in one form or another. Recently I heard it reported that scientists have determined that there actually may be more water below the surface than above, which seems incomprehensible since the oceans are so vast.

In my education overseas, one of the areas of studies was alternative medical studies, namely homeopathy.

Homeopathy is a particularly interesting form of medicine, finding its foundations preempting the pharmaceutical medical industry we find ourselves engulfed in today, by at least two or three thousand years. It has been written in the time of Hippocrates, regarding the ability of "likes curing likes".

Without getting to much into the philosophical or even into medical physiology, the premise is that when you significantly dilute compounds, the resulting compounds can be used to cure the problems caused by the original stronger compounds. For example, arsenic poisoning is treated and cured by giving the patient compounds that have supposedly extremely slight amounts of arsenic in them.

When I was in Europe we had an opportunity to examine not only this process but also samples of these products. I had even on occasion the opportunity to receive homeopathic remedies prescribed right along with the regular pharmaceuticals, and I must admit the healing process not only was faster but often with fewer side effects and downtime.

The process goes something like this; they take the particular poison, compound or substance; arsenic, snake venom, gold, mercury, whatever they happen to want to make into a homeopathic compound, they dissolve it in either pure water or alcohol and then press and sift it to remove solids or impurities.

They then draw out a single drop of the resulting liquid, and place it in a vat, a huge container containing maybe a thousand gallons or so of pure water, an extremely large barrel! This is then thoroughly mixed and a single drop is again drawn out, placed into another vat with water, this process is repeated four to seven times depending on the compound, ending in a final vat of water with what science would say, contains nothing of the original compound, not even a trace.

Yet the resulting water is then drawn out and placed in small vials and distributed to patients who suffer from various particular sicknesses, they take a number of these drops under the tongue, resulting in a cure, and this treatment had been used, with success I might add, for at least the last two thousand years.

I don't know how it is possible, but when we as students tried drops from the various vials, a person could distinctly taste a flavor or essence of the original compound. Each vial had a different distinct taste!

Arsenic being the one I tried, I could really taste the specific almond-like flavor, that is typically found in arsenic poisoning, or at least an after smell in my nose, after tasting the drops, even though I knew that this compound had been diluted to a billionth or maybe even many billions of its original strength.

But I also know that as you continually make half of something even a billion times there is still a small piece left, even a trillion times make something a half or a tenth or a hundredth, there is still a little bit of that ever so small amount left.

The study of Homeopathy would say that a sort of energy exchange is passed into the water from the essence of the compound, and no matter how much you dilute it something from the original is passed through the pure water. The pure water has a property about it that sort of draws out some of the essences of whatever is placed in it and disperses it throughout its entirety. thus the significant cleaning ability of water.

Water makes us clean! Water can purify, sounds Godly to me.

Let us suppose that this is true, science today can only suppose to explain the many energies that not only hold the molecules together, and even surround the various atoms, making them independent of others, though they also know vast distances compared to their individual sizes separate the fractions from their other parts in atoms or molecule.

So if we suppose there is an energy that surrounds and holds these compounds, molecules, and atoms together and makes them into the significant essence they are today, this un-measurable, unexplainable, and even unfathomable energy, (again sound kind of Godly) which is definitely strong and indestructible, being able to be split but not destroyed, then why is it not conceivable that this powerful energy could have an effect on the surrounding like energies it comes in contact with. Energy can not be destroyed only transferred! Hey, scientists say that not me!

And because we do further suppose that this energy can not be destroyed, it can only be transferred as science would teach us, energies of such strength and significance that even just splitting them releases forces that can topple cities as demonstrated at Hiroshima. These yet unknown, un-measurable, unseen, unfelt, only believed to be real by the faith of the observer energies, again seems Godly? These energies that clearly demonstrate some kind of interaction as seen in homeopathy, well this raises all kinds of questions?

If all of this is true, and I have no reason to believe otherwise, then one other fact is true; Jesus's blood was shed, his side was pierced and water gushed out. This was a fact, it was documented and nobody denies this event took place.

What is also fact is that at the moment of His death it is recorded that a great storm irrupted, to the degree where even the many Roman onlookers had to comment; "Surely this was the Son of God", an earthquake that shook the land,

and split the great Jewish temple, ripped the veil, and a rain drenched the land.

But even if it didn't rain we know he was beaten almost unrecognizable, documented! A lot of blood. You would suppose that the area where whipping occurs would have to be washed, eventually!

Any rain or water would mix with his blood, if but a few drops, but all accounts tell us there was a great deal of blood and a great deal of liquid that ushered forth from His side. This, in turn, could flow over the land or soak into the ground, not destroyed only move, it would find its way into the water table eventually, which in turn would find its way to the stream, later rivers and eventually the ocean, where it would be diluted with all of the water of the world.

I guess my point is if a single drop of arsenic can be diluted in a thousand gallon barrel of water, a drop taken from that one, and placed in another vat, over and over again, retaining enough of the essence of the original to heal the person of his infirmity, then I guess it is not inconceivable to believe that the essence of Jesus's blood, the Creator of the entire universe, the healer of all, resides in each and every drop of water we may drink.

"And He said take this cup and drink, for this is the cup symbolizing my blood, take it and think of me"

"When you use water, consume it in your foods, drink it, bath in it, wash the faces of My children with, treat your afflictions with it, if you buy thank me, bless the water with your words, the water will become blessed and in turn release its blessings of healing and life right back into you."

"A promise."

"Water, rainbows, healing, love, they are all the same energies."

Amphorae

A Dream;

I love my children so much, how great is this God of ours who gives so freely and provides the love that just flows from His heart. One night I was praying and an image formed in my mind as clear as the noon daylight.

Yes, my sweet friend I to have had so many visions I could hardly record them as I believe we all do, but for the most part, ignore them, but this one, in particular, was of a large clay vessel that was filled with a liquid.

This liquid is shown with almost a luminescent white light like the purest brightest clear yet white milk or the essence of the white sun itself. The jar or vessel that contained it was one of those old Greek olive oil containers, I can't remember exactly what it was called, but I think it was an amphora or something like that? Anyway, as this amphora filled to the brim, it tips and spills over onto its side, spreading over the whole scene!

As the liquid spreads over the flat dark surface, it forms a sort of pool, an area spreading with ease over the smooth dark yet featureless surface. I can clearly see speckles of light shining from within the liquid, a sort of starlight sparkles', and they then dissipate softly like the remnant of fireworks! Sparklers fading from your vision like the traces left in a dark night as the bright light moves through space, so softly it fades slowly away.

God spoke to me;

"This is how my love is in you!"

"And so is its effect on the world around you!"

"I have one thing you are to do; Love!"

I know how to love, and it seems to have has been held from me for so long, but maybe now that I think of it, by myself!

I have walked in the wilderness, but He has promised that if I follow Him in everything and every way, I will have it back in the portion that which I have lost, multiplied, with interest, as promised!

And He keeps all of His promises!

"Love, healing, light, water, they are all the same, first believe they are real, and realize all the promises are real. Step away from the doubts, lies, and depression that the enemy would deceive you with. Healing is no more difficult than lifting your hand to your mouth an tasting the pure golden sweetness of honey you may have touched."

The First Physical Therapist

Physical Therapy in its most basic form is the application of Physical therapeutic applications as a means to rehabilitate or facilitate the healing process in individuals after they have suffered from an injury, whether it be a traumatic event, a post-acute sickness process or a systemic deviation from the norms of function following one or more breakdown of normal bodily functions, all related to physicality or function.

Practicing Physical Therapy or at least applying the therapeutic techniques to thousands of patients over the course of tens of years, has allowed me to see the relative significance the application of natural stimulus has on the body both in the immediate and long-term regarding the return to normal or even possible enhancement of function. It has also allowed me to witness firsthand where the application of physical stimulus by themselves also result in reduced effectiveness of the applications over a large group of people, thus suggesting for other factors must be involved for a consistent and guaranteed healing outcome that far exceeds the mere prescribed and commonly authorized and practiced procedures.

As I read and studied more the historical accounts of Jesus Christ it occurred to me, increasingly as I looked at them through the eyes of a medical practitioner, that many of the applications of healing had similarities to many of the applications practiced perhaps inadvertently by the majority of the therapeutic practitioners I had witnessed in the field.

"Jesus was the first true healer, healing all parts of the person, not merely the body, but the mind and the spirit simultaneously."

He seemed to be able to discern with Godly intuition exactly the direction in which to apply the necessary stimulus for the more apparent and qualitative result. He knew exactly what direction and in which realm to operate to get the job done.

"This is because He understood people are more than just bodies and symptoms, but also the experiences of their minds, and most importantly their spirits, and in

considering this, applied the healing to all of these areas proportionally according to the individuals need, healing them not only in their immediate physical areas, but completely as to help them on the course to fulfill their own destinies, their very souls."

I have noticed, or better yet have been taught by God, that in every case, some kind of action was coupled with the healing, whether it be *"Pick up your mat and walk"*, *"Go report to the teachers of the temple"*, *"Dip yourselves in the Jordan"* or merely *"Go and sin no more"*, the bottom line there was always an action coupled with healing.

.

"The action places reality into the healing process, not only does the person experience even at the moment a small fraction of improvement, they experience it in their senses; hear, see, and feel, it is through this positive experience that they that they receive a physical momentous experience of healing. There is an exact event created, they have been told and it is now and forever coupled with their own healing experience, they thus believe."

"Belief is the basis for all reality in the world." "I Am is the most powerful force in the entire physical universe,

spiritual, mental, or physical. I Am transcends time and space, for what you believe you are you become."

"If a person only believes even with the most insignificant fraction like a mustard seed, then everything is possible, even the impossible."

"These are not new revelations, everything you need to understand about healing Jesus has already demonstrated, documented and revealed from the very first moment I physically stepped onto the world stage two thousand years ago."

Exercise has the same effect, and that is why it is such a perfect therapeutic tool for rehabilitation of the boy who suffers and needs to pick up his mat and walk. People often misunderstand exercise seeing it as a sort of program one needs to fulfill to accomplish a specific task. But as a therapist I realize that exercise does not cause the body to grow or heal, the body merely reacts to the stimulus that is being given it, that s why it works with some people and with other is doesn't.

If a person wants to walk they merely have to start first believing they are meant to walk, then begin along a path of belief and actions that promotes them to the course of experience which includes walking. Jesus used many examples of exercise, adding movement into the healing process; pick up your matte and walk, go down to the Jordan, go back home your event is already healed. But in my very own practice many seem to do everything they need to do, everything right, suffering from the same issues, some get better and some don't?

"This is because the actual moment of healing took place at the instant Jesus showed up, the rest was the after effect the mopping up of the mess. The person who picked up their matte had to be healed to pick up the matte, they believed what they heard, they felt the results of those words on themselves even if it was but a small fraction, a small mustard seed size portion of faith."

"This belief starts a sort of domino effect a miraculous change in their very genes and spontaneous miracles occur within the bodies anatomical essence moment in time itself."

Sounds like quantum physics, the studying of the most basic particles of the known universe, their movements, interactions and in some cases their possible origins, how does healing fit in here?

"Quantum physics is the study of the particles themselves, the healing takes place within the vast space in them around them and between them."

"If you snap a dry twig at what moment does the twig break? The moment you hear the snap or the moment you feel it?"

"The moment I feel the snap, experience the release of energy, the motion and hear the sound, simultaneously."

"Even in the most sensitive and observant fraction of time it still takes a split second for you to become aware of something after it already occurred, thus the moment is over and forever in the past, leaving you with the feeling of the effect of the action of snapping and the two pieces resting in each hand."

"Sicknesses and injuries are exactly the same, and as well so is healing, they all occur in a moment in time transcending the very essence of time and space. What starts out as simple events become reality depending on your awareness."

"You only become sick after being in an attack if you take it upon yourself and believe it to be so."

"My children were not created sick, they can only claim that on themselves, or have it placed upon them in the form of a curse."

"What doesn't kill you makes you stronger!"

PETER J COLLA

You Have Not Because You Ask Not

"When dealing with storms in our life, I give you everything you need to overcome any challenge, you merely have to look, reach out and take what I have already given you to overcome."

Back to the statement of "What doesn't kill us makes us stronger" seems to find itself the least applicable in the annals of medicine. While it is a common statement throughout the world and generally believed with only the slightest resistance, especially when people as a whole understand this statement and its application to the body as well as our life as a whole, as a medical provider especially in the past, I would probably be more on the opposite side of the fence stating when it comes to medical issues, sicknesses, especially tragic cases of injuries afflicting a large parts of the body or multiple systems, the opposite is more often true, what doesn't kill us often leaves us so dilapidated, we wish we were dead.

But I am here to tell you, it is my experience after treating thousands of individuals, what doesn't actually kill them at the time of the injury, does lead to making them stronger one hundred percent of the time.

A person might say; "Well what about when a person loses a leg, what then? How are they possibly stronger?"

It doesn't matter what you think you lose, that kind of thinking especially when it comes to functions of the body, is equivalent to concentrating on what you do not have, rather than looking at what you do. Living in the past, dwelling on what you have lost, or looking at what you don't have basically is the same as staring at the shadows.

"When you start looking at what is, rather than what is not you will find everything you need is right in front of you."

"Tell me about Todd."

I had a friend his name was Todd, larger than life, he was an ex-professional athlete, in his prime over six foot six, well over two hundred and eighty pounds of muscle, power, and arrogant grit. You would have to be if you wanted to play professional sports, especially in a profession where everyone is trying to throw you on your back, humiliate you, and step over you as they push forward toward their own goals. Which seems, more often than not, to have to go right through you to get where they want to go!

Todd suffered from severe diabetes which he had no problem admitting or stating was his own fault not taking care of his own body all those years of college and later in professional sports. Too much of everything, most of which he knew was not good for him now seemed to cost him dearly. Todd slowly lost first the feeling in his feet, only later to begin to lose circulation in first the toes, and then progressively up until it resulted in him having to have both legs amputated in multiple and ever increasingly frequent surgeries to eventually lose both legs well above both knees.

One day he rolls in his athletic wheelchair with two temporary prosthetic legs strapped to the back, carrying a prescription to learn to walk with the legs. He was a good friend and it had been a while since I saw him so I enthusiastically said to him; "So are we going to learn how to use your legs?"

He said with angry dismay; "No! Those things are not my legs, I lost my legs, I came here to if you could help me with this pain that will not stop killing me, and it's right there!" As he pointed to the foot peddle out in front of the chair where his foot should have been. Phantom pain was quite common with amputations, but no matter what we did for his remaining leg or his back as to calm the nerve pain, nothing seemed to help.

At that time we had son of my own martial arts instructor, John working for us as a student assistant. A 3rd degree black-belt himself, so I thought it would at least be fun for Todd to work with him, and he quickly took a liking to the boy, Todd not thinking much of martial arts, and often said only girls used their feet to fight. Todd would sit there and playfully try to slap at John who had no problem blocking or dodging the various almost comical antics the larger man threw at him. This relationship went on for about a week or maybe two before Todd stopped coming in.

Then John finally told me about a month later that Todd found it so interesting the ability to defend himself from a chair John displayed, as well as being completely surprised to hear there were entire areas of martial arts instruction that did nothing more than teach a person how to defend themselves from a chair. Todd started showing up at Johns father's studio where they would roll his wheelchair out onto the mats and teach him chair-bound martial arts! Todd loved it so much he came in three to four times a week regularly now.

"That's great," I said and didn't think anything more about it until Todd walked in the office three or four months later, walking on his prosthetics, no crutches, no cane!

"Todd! My God" I said, "You look great! Who taught you to walk so fast?" He walked in and sat down in a chair in front of me, a smile on his face and didn't say a word until I sat down myself in front facing him. At the moment I sat, my own foot slid out slightly and accidentally kicked his prosthetic leg.

"Why did you kick my leg?" He said

I never answered him, I was interested in how good he looked. The significances of his question to me I would not understand until only recently in my career, years later.

"I want to thank you." Todd said with a smile and went on, "I was here before I lost my legs," as he held out his arm at about stomach height.

"After I lost my legs, I was here!" As he put his hand down nearly to the ground holding it down there. "I was down, low, and ready to just about give it up."

"But then I started studying martial arts with John, and went to here." As he raised his hand high above his head and held it there. "When I began to study the Martial Arts, walking (as he lowered his hand back to the place it was to start with) didn't seem like such a difficult thing to do anymore."

For years to come, I used Todd's story to emphasize the significance of doing something greater than the task being prescribed as a means to accomplish it; like a person learning to walk by learning to dance, or someone learning the balance of back muscles by studying Tai-Chi. But the most significant moment of the story eluded me until just recently.

When Todd first came in he said; "I'm not wearing those things, they are not my legs I lost my legs." Now he said; "Why did you kick my leg"? He got his legs back and in the process became a Martial Artist. Todd would later go on to do many things he had never done earlier, skiing, parachuting, diving, all things gained in his new found desire to venture out and conquer since he already had become a conqueror.

"Todd was a great man with a great calling, he walked through life perhaps walking the wrong direction, lost his legs, but found them again, and through this experience, he became a conqueror and now he flies."

The why is still so difficult to stomach, and sometimes it is easy to see why some people would actually want to die than go on?

"Many people long for death long before the peacefulness is granted, some people even understand the essentialness of results, these being an accumulation of actions all the paths and adventurer's along the way may bring. When a young person who longs for just another bright day is suddenly faced with the realization of tragic and definite dreams incomplete, it seems to often be received with a tear."

"The perplexity of understanding the complexities of the failures of the body, or the reasons one or another is faced with sudden and inescapable life-ending tragedy requires an understanding that transcends the ability to understand granted in the limitations of this life."

"For now the question on the table; You have not because you ask not?"

"You have not, because you ask not, and you ask not, because you chose not to look for the answers that grant

you wisdom in the direction in which it was designed to demonstrate."

"Jesus demonstrated immediately and purely for those who looked to God, just looked that direction, in a path, or eye, or ear, and even just in touch, simple rain fell in the form of healing upon every one of their heads freely regardless of their histories, races, or even religions."

"All anyone had to do was, is, and will always be but ask. Look to towards Him, if even but a touch of the hem of His garment and they know they would receive healing."

First people have to pull their own heads out from under the veils of the lies and deceits of the world, the accumulation of a lifelong series of programming, misguided teaching and spoon fed poisoning to even contemplate something might actually be different then we have been told. I guess death is the finish line moment of when life is complete or not?

"If your race is over then you will not be able to overcome, but if you merely survive the ordeal and live to another day and healing has already occurred, it is you that realizes the

truth within the image you experience, then decides what to do about the messes the storms make."

"If I make you a promise, you can count on it, you can bank on it, you can bet your life on it, you can bet the farm, all wonderful terms you yourselves have created to add solid perspective to promises carved in stone, created and everlasting by Me."

"I already said energy is everlasting, death is merely a consequence of turning away from Me, like other stone in your garden they are merely momentary places you rest your feet upon as you step through the everlasting path of your soul, a promise."

"Promises made, promises fulfilled, I show you this with the appearance of signs if you but take a moment stop and look. The promises of the rainbows, listen to the birds for they are my messengers in Earthly form instructed to bring messages of hope and peace to those who would but stop and listen, raindrops on the faces of my children, a reminder of the free waters I give to everyone who but look up, snowflakes; winters cold crystalized into perfected *realizations that every single one is different and specific for you."*

"You want to be healed, look up and ask."

Belief

"If you are going to experience healing in its fullest or even embrace the healing I have promised you then a good first step is the stepping stone of belief. You must be willing to believe, or at the very least accept the notion that it may be true."

"Belief is the greatest portion of life, it is the greatest portion of healing."

I must say that with the majority of people I have treated throughout my career, the belief at least resolving around the prospect of success with healing is a product largely dependent on the persons own personal belief. This too has changed over the course of the last thirty years, people through the media or education from the internet draw their own conclusions about the prognosis of the injury they are suffering from.

Having this information, while many would think is good, also when speaking doubt into their lives gives them increased hopelessness because if they happen to read there is nothing that can be done for a particular ailment, regardless of what I might say they already have become convinced regarding what think is the truth.

"A person has to believe or at least be willing to believe they can be healed, or perhaps deserve to be healed." "How many people come to you with the predisposed idea that they are receiving exactly what they deserve either by actions by themselves or even just by the heritage of their birth?"

I would say the majority, all if I had to be honest, every single person I had ever treated where the subject actually came up, when they actually took responsibility, with the exception of children, or had what they felt was a predisposed origin for the affliction they were suffering, all uniformly believed they suffer as a result of their own path or actions, and in almost every case felt that is why they remained ill. While others would heal, or escape the persecution these sicknesses seemed to cause, they would in most case say approximately the same thing, I did it to myself, I did this or that, played this or that sport, partied too much, walked down this or that path I knew I shouldn't and that why I have this today, and why others get better and I don't. You have no idea what I have done!

"To a degree they are right, the majority of afflictions could be avoided by choosing of specific paths in life or not, but the idea of not deserving healing falls right in line with the misconception of deserving forgiveness or not. This right is the gift granted to each and every person through the death of my son."

"People will ask for forgiveness for things, especially when they clearly know they are doing wrong at the moment and chose this direction anyway. They will also forgive others, especially if they are for the most part good in their hearts, even enemies or people who have done horrible wrongs towards them, but where people, in general, have the greatest amount of issue is forgiving themselves, this holds back healing often more than anything? They speak with their thoughts and prayers; Lord please heal my diabetes, which is no different then; remove me from this storm I am suffering from as I continue to go down this road towards what I know is dark clouds."

"If you listen very closely to what is being said; "Lord Heal" and then "My Diabetes" on one hand they want to overcome it and on the other they claim it!"

You can't have both, and as children who are created in the image of God; your words have power, it was written in my Word; That you will be accountable for your every word, a Promise and a truth.

"Tell me what you know about Michelle?"

Michelle

I love to use as the example of the power of belief when relating a story told to me by my wife Anna regarding her friend Michelle. Michelle personally gave Anna permission to use her name and example when helping other people, so I will use her real name.

Michelle was a client of Anna during the time she was teaching Pilates in Amsterdam and was a loyal attendant of the class for many years, and as many such friendships develop they became more friends then just instructor and client. After a great deal of time Michelle came in one day and said to Anna; "I will not be coming into Pilates anymore."

When Anna pressed her to find out why Michelle finally broke down and shared with her that she had been struggling with bone and blood cancer for years, and recently she had seen the doctor and heard it had returned to the highest stage 4. She would have to start soon the most aggressive form of chemotherapy at least twenty treatments in six months, and it would probably leave her completely incapacitated.

The most difficult question was asked; "What are your chances?" The doctors said with the chemo, she had six months, without it, it could be only weeks?

After much crying, as many friends would do, the question was posed; "Have you tried absolutely everything?"

And while Michelle assured her she had, she was willing to look once again in any possible alternative. Calling all of her friends and searching endless hours in alternative healing there in Holland and abroad, they finally came across one spiritual healer they had until then not heard of.

A spiritual healer in Brazil that claims to examine the patient and then pray, and whatever God tells him to have the patient do, they are instructed to do. So they thought what can it hurt let's call him. At first, the healer stated they would have to come in front of him for the process to work, but for Michelle, the thought of traveling all the way to Brazil was too much, so they thanked the healer but couldn't come. He felt pity for the two women and said; "I never do this but go ahead and send me your picture and I will try to pray while looking at it and see if God says anything to me."

After receiving the picture he called them back and said to the two women this is what I was told; *"Put on a pure white gown and lie down in bed, pray to God to open your eyes, and whoever you see, whatever they have done, pray to God to forgive them, even if with only words. And this is the most important part; forgive yourself for your part in this problem."*

"I hope this helps, God bless." He hung up.

The two ladies went out and bought the white cloths, and while they didn't lie down on the bed they did go to the ocean and scream out loud, crying and praying.

Michelle was Vietnamese one of the Boat-People from the late sixties early seventies, coming to America with her mother. While she remembered scattered memories of her past, she, like many other women with traumatic upbringing, really had little or no memories of her childhood, as a matter of fact, the time before coming to America she had absolutely no memories, being a complete blank, even though she was nearly eleven when she arrived. But suddenly as these prayers and tears rang out she suddenly started remembering vivid and complete memories of her childhood she had locked away so many years earlier.

She suddenly began to remember being systematically and repeatedly raped by her father and uncle, and many of his friends for years, all the way back to being a very little child. What made things worse, is that she also remembered that when she tried to tell her mother, she was immediately and repeatedly silenced as to not bring shame upon their family.

It was commonly known by many people that Michelle had her whole life been ashamed of being Vietnamese, but it wasn't until this moment did she understand why she always hated her blood, and even her heritage, her very bones!

They quickly remembered the instruction of the Brazilian Healer to forgive whoever came to mind even if it is with words only, as difficult as it was. *"Mouth the words out loud if nothing else."* This whole process seemed to take all afternoon as the faces of all the assailants began to rush across her memory and each needing in their turn to be forgiven one after another.

They finally finished at the sea and went back to Anna's apartment where Michelle was so exhausted from the ordeal she just wanted to lay down. As all the memories flooding in finally brought her up to the age and point where she had active adult memories, and consequentially all the forgiveness words were spoken, Anna reminded her "now you have to also forgive yourself," perhaps the hardest thing one can be asked to do.

Michelle spoke out the words of forgiveness of herself for hating her own life, her blood, her heritage, her very bones, and forgave herself for her self hatred. At the very moment she just spoke those final words through the tears and sobs, she suddenly fell back in the bed asleep, seemingly completely exhausted from the work.

After the second day straight of Michelle not waking up Anna began to be concerned, checking up with her, but she seemed to be sleeping soundly and decided not to wake her. After nearly three days of non-stop sleep suddenly she woke up, she looked better and more rested then she had appeared the entire time Anna knew her. As a matter of fact, she stated she had never felt better.

The first chemo appointment was scheduled for the following Friday, and as was customary she had to go in for tests to make sure the dosage was correct. Upon completing the first test the doctor was baffled by the result; it showed absolutely no trace of cancer in her blood. It was so low, basically zero, that he ordered the test taken two more times at two different labs, just to make sure his own equipment or test wasn't faulty, all with the same result.

The cancer had vanished! Not only had it vanished but she had absolutely not a single trace of any cancer whatsoever own her body.

I would like to say this story had a happy ending, but the doctors not believing even the results of their own test still forced Michelle with the threat of cancelation of her insurance to continue the chemo regiment anyway, stating that perhaps the cancer is merely hidden?

A few months later Michelle died of complications from pneumonia, she developed while on the chemo.

"As you can see the single most powerful weapon on the planet in the spiritual realm is forgiveness, and forgiving yourself is absolutely essential for any assurance of the healing process will be manifested and more importantly completed, of this point, we will discuss later."

Why did Michelle have to die? Would her life have not been much more of an inspiration and being able to tell such he story herself?

"She did tell it herself and is an inspiration, this is the true definition of a Martyr's death."

"While Michelle knew where the mess was in her life, she never examined the actual causes until right before the end."

She still died?

"Yes, and her purpose had been fulfilled, to teach Anna and through her, you the significance of Forgiveness in the

healing process. Forgiveness is one of the most powerful weapons of cleansing and life you have been given."

"Why some people die and others don't, specifically why did Michelle have to die then, for the same reason your first wife and child died when they did because it was their time. Remember what you wrote about the flower vision?"

"You are all flowers to me."

We Are All Flowers

One of the earliest memories I had regarding a speaking word or thought from God, and writing it down, came very shortly after the first word I received, and had a marked effect on me directly and for years to come. I remember stating perhaps in my prayer and maybe even out loud to God; "So if You would that everyone would be healed, what is stopping them, why do only a few seemed to be healed?"

"What is the difference? Why do some have miracles, and some don't? Especially when they, and I, all seem to be asking?"

I asked that question, didn't get much of an answer, yet at the very moment I asked it, in my mind an image of a beautiful Tuscan landscape came in front of my eyes, filled my vision painting a landscape with beautiful colors; reds, purples, whites, and greens, flowing winds cascading across the fields as it gently flowed in the summers breeze. A solitary tree standing in the center, strong and picturesque, like a guarding sentinel protecting all under its reaching arms.

A few months later I was hiking with a nurse friend who upon hearing my story of the passing of my first wife and child in a car accident, promptly told me of her own experience of the passing of her child while still a baby.

As comforting as it was, it was rare for me to speak to someone regarding the loss of my spouse or child, or in this case both. The only people that seemed to understand, were people who went through such losses themselves, prompting me to not only talk about it with her, but also to write of the account very early on in my writing career.

This is from that writing;

I knew a man once, a long time ago, he was a younger man, naive yet full of faith. Faith in God but also in the world! This man always loved God, even walked and talked with Him his whole life, but often knew not how to show it.

Then one day he found himself in a far-off land, and the last thing he expected happened; God decided to bless him by allowing our young traveler to meet one of God's "Truly wonderful flowers"!

It didn't take long for this man to fall in love with the flower, because everyone who ever met her loved her. But another true miracle occurred, she actually loved him as well! Giving up school, home, family, even country, in a place that didn't speak his language, for a gift given by God didn't seem like a sacrifice at all, but more a privilege.

Days and nights filled with laughter, most of the time at nothing at all, coupled with the sweet scent of fresh dew on newly blossomed flowers, misty morn of a cool spring day, so was her breath. A touch so soft yet graced with strength, that it lit a flame in this man's heart that encircled said heart as gently as a warm feather bed snuggles shoulders on a cold winters night.

Every curl, every curve, the every glance, her mere touch was as perfect as the speckling of beauty marks on her legs that randomly adorned her being like the stars of the sky. Perfect, maybe not by worlds standards, but to him as perfect as any glorious creation his young eyes had yet witnessed.

How sweet it was to sit across a crowded room and have her look at him, mouth a word, and he would know exactly everything she said. How sweet was it to come from a feast every day that was her, and be so full he couldn't even glance at another morsel.

She was his love, she was his heart, she was his friend, she was his life. She was his wife!

A man would risk, even sacrifice his life gladly to protect the precious pearl that God has blessed him with. She does as well; risks her own, sacrificing body, risking life to joyfully bring a child into the world.

Blessings beyond imagination!

Some would say our young traveler had it all when you have everything you need all the extras are just extra and really only amount to simple pleasures that rain down from God as simple flakes of snow in a perfect winters scene.

But suddenly one day which should have been glorious, being only a single one before the scheduled day of birth of their second child, beauty turns to tragedy! A stranger who would rush to beat a red light would cross her path, and life for her, as well as the child, would disappear from her blue eyes.

To understand the depth of what he experienced, only those that have experienced similar losses can feel the pain, and through this common feeling, this kind of tragic experience, can one relate to what he went through after that horrific day.

When I say those of similar loss, I mean someone who has a part of themselves taken from this world. Not to diminish anyone's loss, whether it is a parent, a dear friend, or close loved one, but nothing seems to compare to the loss of a spouse or child! This may very well be due to the fact that a child is created with a piece of ourselves. In the same way, when two people become one flesh as is the case in marriage, in some cases they become one person.

The loss of either of these kinds of individuals in our lives can leave us not only depressed at this loss but left with a sense of utter and unexplainable incompleteness. We feel like a part of us is missing, and no matter what we do, we can't seem to find a fill to that lost part!

Why he asked?!!!

Our young traveler, our angry, confused, guilt-ridden, tired young believer, would enter the wilderness! Wander with fist-in-air, kicking rocks, head down, eyes turned away from the glare of a day that has become various shades of grey.

Days turned into weeks, which turned into years. Relationships came and went, and with them came various levels of betrayal even from those who pledged there deepest devotion.

Funny how a man can just slowly walk into a "Death Valley," slowly descending, unknowingly, most of the time, until he finds himself so far below the "Sea" level, that he can hardly imagine a way out. When all seems lost and giving up becomes something our blessed, not so young man possibly looks at for the first time in his life, finally, out of desperation, he calls out to Jesus for help and Jesus answers! In a bathtub of all places!

The climb out is a rapid ascent when God shows us the path! Three things happen when you get to the other side, at the top of the mountain ridge that crests the edge of the valley; one, you can look back and see the whole valley, giving a clear picture of the whole and what exactly it was, and two, it doesn't look so big as it did when you where deep in, and third, a person might even thank Him for the experience of overcoming, the task won, the lesson learned!

God is so good! Not only does He rescue His child when called, but He also blesses our traveler with the answer to his "why?" question that has haunted him all the years of his wilderness walk.

One day he was asked by a female friend who had also had a tragic loss of a child. When she heard of his loss she turned, with tears in her eyes said; "If God loves as you say He does, then how do you explain the loss of an innocent person such as your wife or child, or my baby?"

At this point, our new recruit in Gods army had become a "Believer" and knew Jesus lived in his heart, but the answer to that question he had never quite heard!

He closed his eyes and asked God for wisdom. God spoke in his mind. "Well, you said we could ask anything and it would be given?" "So I am asking?"

An image immediately appeared;

He softly speaks into her ear; "I just had the vision of a beautiful field of flowers, mostly reds, but also yellows, violets, and whites, appear in my mind. In the middle of a sweeping hill lined valley meadow stood a shady tree, quite inviting and peaceful! You know the kind they show on a travel brochure to Tuscany, Italy or someplace like that?"

"Peaceful, restful, perfect in order and design, balanced majesty of symphonic grace as the breeze gently flows over blossoms, like the caressing waves of a green-tinted shore."

"The heard the voice of God just say in my head;"

"Consider the flowers;"

"Some lie in the middle of the field, where the Sun is strong and the soil is deep, plenty of water, safe."

"Some lie under the tree's, a good safe place but not as much sun, they just don't seem to grow as well."

"Some lie in the rocks, where the soil is thin and water spars, they do not grow well at all, a seemingly poor life."

"Some lie in the weeds, where life is hard and struggle seems to be a daily event, their short life choked out sometimes cruelly."

"And some lie on the road, where the wagon comes by and snuffs out their life suddenly!"

"You are all those flowers in that field! You are all flowers to me; some you are strong, some of you are weak, some of you are tall, some are small, all equal, all loved, all perfect."

"Yours is not to understand why this one lies here, or that one there, in my most perfect field, yours is to Thank Me, for the time you got spend with my most precious flowers!"

Our young believer then understood and had an overwhelming realization that he needed to "thank God" for two things; for all the precious time he got to spend in his life with such a beautiful creation as one of God's precious flowers, his wife and even unborn child. If it was but a moment, it was infinitely better then to have never had known them at all! And two; that God loves him enough to let me see the rest of the beauty of this gift we call our life, seeing not only our place in it, but his hand in every sight, sound, taste, and breath we share. If God didn't have all of the flowers in their perfect place, and in their perfect color, we wouldn't have the even more glorious field!

The true picture of life, as He sees it, and as we experience it.

This traveler was me!

God is faithful, I have had precious time with one of His most precious flowers.

That was many years ago, praise God I have also had since been promised restoration, and God always keeps His promises.

A flower?

Could God have another for me, and allow me to be one for her!

"Yes"

The Real Power in Prayer

This statement of *"Yes"* was then followed by a time of utter and complete silence and other than confirmations that God actually speaks to each of us constantly and continually, we merely have the choice whether or not to take our attention from the concerns of the day, actually listen seemed to be the theme of the moment. Silence as to what exactly the true therapy was or how did it perpetuate itself was only up for interpretation at this time.

So I tried prayer, and while I never actually prayed out loud to a single one of my patients, I would, under my breath, pray for them as I worked on them. I even over the course of the following couple of months tried praying and then see if they could actually feel the difference or not.

While I never considered myself much of a praying person, my own Christian upbringing seemed to embed into my mind at least a blueprint of how it should actually go, at least I hoped. Most of the time the prayer was more or less me asking for something from God, not completely different from the more than a few times I had prayed throughout my own life. But for the most, the actual prayer amounted to little more than myself quietly asking God to bless the person I was working for, heal them or take away their pain. That was basically all I could seem to muster.

I was amazed to realize that often the patients themselves could actually feel something and on many occasions would ask me "Are you doing something different, because suddenly it feels so much better?" This in itself was perplexing and fascinating, both in itself. But still I was wondering often regarding the patients, especially while speaking of immediate and reducing pain or tension, these reported reductions only lasting hours or momentary relief just to have the symptoms return shortly after they left the building or at least until the next day, did the prayer do anything or did it just amount to a sort of placebo effect even in my own treating method?

"People have no idea the power in prayer, next to love it is the most powerful force in the entire universe. You have no idea the life giving and life taking effects your very words have. Let me show you a glimpse."

"Crisis is a storm?"

Being in a place of acceptance even if this is just a spiritual place, and not just the passing social/economical moments of our lives, can and always seems to leave us in a position of vulnerability that pulls at the very strings of our mind and soul. That feeling of uncertainty, accountability, openness, trends us to question our own stability in an already unstable world.

It is no wonder why everyone hates crisis, not to mention the usual resulting manifesting conflicts that always seem to fill us with dread, fear, and a deep feeling of insignificance, makes us stand back and look at ourselves often with resulting realization of how small we really are. This, of course, plays havoc with our self-esteem and/or the lack thereof, making us just cherish every moment we live in crisis (I was being facetious), bringing to mind the scripture *"consider yourself glad when you are being persecuted"*! This is a very difficult situation and concept to wrap our arms around. How can we possibly count ourselves glad when we are in crisis? The answer; knowing that there is an opportunity for change and through this change, we can become a better person.

I am no stranger to crisis, and if anyone knows me they also realize that crisis has been my middle name over the course of the last forty or so years. Thank God for this crisis, for it is through these many crisis situations that God has truly done a work in my life.

A great line from the movie The Shawshank Redemption, the narrating character remembers a quote from his friend "You can get started living, or you can get on started dying?"

I believe in any true crisis, we find ourselves at one pivotal point where we must choose to "get busy living, or get busy dying", this choice, whether we want to admit it or not, often manifests' itself in the active drawing close to God or a departure from him. Death is what waits for us if we depart from Him!

I'd like to think that I have chosen wisely, and I am drawing closer to Him then away, but at the same time, realizing that He is all around us and in us; it is myself that will somehow on a spiritual level draws closer or move away. Now that presents itself with a difficult dilemma, how do we move away from something that completely and utterly surrounds and comprises every aspect of the world we live in, including us! It would seem that it would be like jumping in a pool and then just by a pure act of will, or choice, decide we don't want to be wet!

I'd like to think I ponder, on a regular basis such philosophical thoughts, but to be honest I have a hard time contemplating whether or not I should water the trees in my yard, let alone my place in the universe in reference to God.

It is for this reason that I believe God gives us visions and dreams, if He had to wait around for us meager Humans to ponder a deep thought, especially in this age where we are being bombarded with every aspect of mind-numbing, psycho-distractions, I believe He'd be waiting until He was blue in the face, which He could be right now, who really knows the face of God? My point is in the muck and mire I call my life at this particular moment, God in his infinite grace gave me a vision. And while the interpretation eluded me, and may still elude me to its full extent, I feel God wanted me at least to write it down.

This is the full account of the "Prayer Vision" and how it was discerned to me, or at least what it has meant to me personally;

Amazing as it is in the case of my life, whenever I feel I have little desire to do something of which I am actually being told to do either by God, a parent or someone in authority over me, a nudging by my own laziness or hard-headedness seems to prompt me first not to do it. And actually, most of the time, these thing's I finally reluctantly do anyway actually after the fact materialize into a realization they are probably good for me in the first place. Usually, these particular activities in these particular moments, are exactly what I'm supposed to do, and it turns out, that in many cases it would seem that God has something very good in store for me, if I decide to do them anyway!

So was the case of a particular invitation to a men's prayer meeting 6:30 am on a Tuesday morning when I really had little or no desire to get out of bed. It was my first of such prayer meetings, and I didn't feel particularly at home or did I expect to get anything too significant out of it. I have never been much of a prayer, having never been taught, (Catholic school upbringing), and if I was, I certainly was either not paying attention, or didn't remember.

But with much prompting I decided to go and as it began to draw an end the men decided, or maybe this is a regular occurrence, to close with prayer. In typical fashion, I closed my eyes, and maybe even started to agree with the prayers of the leader or other men that chimed in.

At this particular moment a different man spoke and for some unknown reason, I turned my head without opening my eyes to look at the man speaking. This was a bit unusual for me because it wasn't like I was expecting to see anything in the darkness of my closed eyes. But to my amazement I did see something; coming from the direction of the man I was looking at, I could see in my closed-eye landscaped darkness a distinct wave action emanating from his direction.

Pulsating from a distinct point, his point, and radiating up and out, almost in a wave-like fashion of a pond or something, except still dark, I almost had the impression I was looking into a dark pool on a clear dark night, and someone was throwing stones into the pond. Waves moving out, but mostly up. This wave created an almost uniform undulation in the blackness of my eyesight, or lack thereof, creating only slight shades of black with very dark grays.

I sat there and stared for quite a moment, which seemed like a long moment. Thankfully the man leading the prayer was a bit long-winded, because I had time to turn my head to the direction of the other men, those next to the one I first noticed, the others to my other side, and even the leader in front of me, realizing that each was creating his own sets of waves. They were each on their own pulsating tempo, and with their own strengths, and as I sat in amazement, I began to realize that all of the wave patterns were slowly starting to assimilate into one, a single greater and very directed large wave, and this wave was pulsating at such an intensity that I could almost physically feel the pulses in my body, especially as I became aware that they were coming. Kind of like the soft reverberations a person feels from the base during a concert.

The wave continued and that was the only thing I could see in the vast darkness of my closed-eyed vision, but suddenly the enormous wave began to lose strength and eventually dissipated to nothing, only moments shortly prior to the conclusion of the prayer. I later shared the sight, vision, whatever, with my then teacher and very close friend Robert, but the meaning of the experience was not clearly brought to me until much later, ever days and weeks.

God spoke to me through many words including verbal confirmations, spoken words, written words, preached, taught, every sort of very Godly people and friends in my life, and even the "still soft voice" that I should listen to the most, but which admittedly, I ignore more than hear myself.

In clarifying the vision, God basically said; *"All that you see, all that you touch, all that you hear, taste, smell, feel, is not the real world, but the things you don't see, feel, touch, hear, or taste are truly the real things".*

And as I pondered this, He spoke to many other examples and how they play into the spiritual battles that are constantly waging around us unseen! *"For we do not battle against flesh and bone, but against principalities and forces unseen..."*

"For example; you are created in the image of God, and with that, fortunately also comes a responsibility of being a creator yourselves. That one fact being "creator" sets you apart from all other creations. The entire universe was set into creation with the spoken word! You confess your salvation before Man with the spoken word. You will be accountable for every "Word" that is uttered out of your mouth. And many more examples of where the word; "Word" is mentioned as a powerful and creative force."

Now scientists will tell us that energy cannot be created or destroyed and if this is the case, what happens to all of those spoken words that we have ever uttered? Do they just disappear, or as scientists may state with energy, and maybe even God verifies (as if He needs to verify anything a man should speculate), that it just keeps going, ever-weakening in effect, weaker and weaker as they dissipate, in essence settling into the environment around precipitating over time less of an influence on the things around them then they may initially, yet half of even a very small amount is still half?

Never quite gone, always having some effect on the world around us, our family, friends, this chair, ourselves, forever accountable! So maybe like the prayer, our words are real things, animate, real creations in an unseen world, but because we don't see the effect on the in-animate, on that rock or on that wall, we assume they have no effect. But the effect, like the real action in the experiential world, is a real effect in the unseen world.

How significant in our real or seen world are the effects of things that are unseen? The effect of love, hate, slander, radiation, poisonous gas, phobia's, too much sun, too little sun, a flirting glance from a beautiful woman, a judgmental look from a boss or teacher, the poker face or lack thereof, a smile, a babies breath, a lover's scent, the statement to a child "your stupid", your pretty, your fat, you're a genius, being told you have cancer, or that someone is proud of you? Many of these types of unseen entities, words, waves, can have a life-changing effect for years even into generations, much more than permanent than even a baseball bat to the same head.

Well, if that be the case, maybe we can take it one step further, and when we do something we know is wrong, is it possible that it's not just an arbitrary event. Often believing that if we don't hurt anyone, or nobody sees the harm in it, that it doesn't have a lasting and permanent effect?

Maybe, just maybe, we are creating entities in the spiritual world, real anomalies that just kind of gather around us, almost like spiritual dark balloons, or bricks, or something maybe even more dark, sinister, and not so desirable, that over time, and with enough accumulations, these things have the ability to isolate us from all who we love; God, our spouses, our children, everything good in the world even, ourselves. We become enveloped and saturated with dark!

A single glimpse of porn may not lead to a divorce, but coupled with many visitations to internet porn sites, might later facilitate a justification of dabbling in chat, and even later maybe a secret meeting with some other lonely darkened sole looking for companionship or something, sitting in the same dilemma not knowing where to look or at what. We might just find ourselves completely surrounded and engulfed in these dark bricks or dark balloons to the point where we can hardly breath, divorce not only becomes a viable option but the only choice!

We can find examples of this in all forms of short-lived gratification; drugs, hate, theft, alcohol drinking, sexual promiscuity, self mutilation, overeating, all forms and kinds of sin, perpetrated against ourselves, creating around us an atmosphere of darkness and seclusion that may ultimately result in murmuring, blaspheming, pride, even suicide, the ultimate act of self hatred! When all is dark, why continue? How sad that in most cases it was our own hand that built every dark brick, every bit of straw and mud, one spoon, one puff, one look, one piece of stone at a time.

But praise Jesus when He says; *"If you ask for forgiveness, I will place that sin as far away as the East is from the West!"* Why, does God have to move it away if it doesn't exist, if it is just some insignificant, invisible event in the past? Is He actually picking up something real and moving it!

But if one is true, could the opposite be true also, we should also examine the other side of the coin; Love! When we love our neighbor as ourselves, when we do a kind unselfish thing for our neighbor, our spouse, our children, strangers, our enemies, maybe we are creating something substantial in the heavenly realm, something that has a lasting effect on the entire universe, something that can't be taken from us, something that we may even take with us in death?

Acts of obedience, when done for the Heavenly Father all have to be acts of love! Maybe we are building that spiritual temple that mansion that we, as created in the image of God, may possess also.

"For all the commandments, the greatest of these is love." When we speak of Jesus, we minister or witness is it not said; *"this can only be done through the Holy Spirit, which is Love in us." And is it also said that; "Love can only come from God!"*

Maybe this is what is meant by; *"storing your treasures up in heaven, where there is no rust, no worm to eat, or no thief to steal. For where your treasure there your heart will be also."*

What a wonderful thought; to think that with each loving, a kind and good word spoken from our mouths, or the very actions of our lives we are creating something total and indestructible, indestructible in the unseen but real universe.

If the spoken word has such creative power, and love has its own creative manifestations, what about the combination of the two, resulting in praise and worship? What a powerful effect that the combination of these two creative powers manifests, and it is no wonder why the Lord basks in the praises of His people! Did he not say that even the angels stop and take notice, and God himself turns His face towards the praises of His people!

He created us in his image and then so desires for us to express ourselves in a way that demonstrates our true master design.

It becomes a bit scary to think that with every action, that might not be particularly of God, we can be creating a negative influence in the universe as well.

This realization manifested itself into a bit of release from me also, into the realization and significance of forgiveness when a person creates a significant amount of black entities around themselves, they begin then to become trapped in their private dark hell they have created, it becomes impossible for them to find love or have a loving act in that secluded place. As if the darkness blocks the light from getting in. Forgiveness is, in essence, a sledgehammer to knock down the wall of darkness we all create around us.

It also became understandable how flesh, or the desire for darkness, would dominate in such a situation, and the spirit desiring good would be weak or nearly non-existent. I often wondered how some self-proclaimed people of faith regardless of the religious name could confess Christ or God, and still act so dark towards each other?

I say a release for me, because when I think about a person engulfed in a quagmire or dark slime, built up with many layers of bricks, mortar, and filth, that has accumulated over years, months, days, or even a moment, it takes away the personal aspect of their attack, and kind of shows me where the real blame for this poor sole rests, making it much easier to hate the sin but love the sinner! To forgive!

Forgiveness an act of love, and the very act of placing away from us, in the same way, God places away from himself sin; it is so comprehensible how the effect of the sin loses its hold on our immediate world. And while we often feel at the time, we are doing someone else such service or a self-sacrificing act, in reality, we are doing something for ourselves that not only benefits us directly, but also the world immediately surrounding us.

In this way, we also set down a hedge of protection around our family and friends and everyone we pray for, forgive and love. We build fortresses around all of the people we love, making it possible for them to experience love much easier than without our efforts. All of this through the miraculous gift of mercy, forgiveness, grace, and love; the greatest gift of God!

"So is it with sicknesses removing the darkness that you have surrounded yourself with allows then the light to shine through and the sickness must flee."

Jerry

Belief is so strong, and I have seen so many examples of people believing what they are told, even to the point of experiencing physical effects merely because their mind tells them it is so.

One particularly extreme example is with Uncle Jerry.

A man healthy his whole life, an Army Ranger, a survivor of countless battles in World War II, he even was one of the few that can say they stormed Normandy Beach and survived, comes home and starts his life. Becomes a professional football player, merely because of his size and strength, not the success or fame of today because in those days playing meant jumping on a train to go play on the weekend, leather helmet and few dollars pay, but whatever you are strong, big and its fun.

He lives a good life, a trade of his hands, married, children, the home, car, and dog, cabin in the woods, soon he would retire and finally relax into the life of comfortable leisure he had hoped for, perhaps longed for, for, oh, so many years.

He is a man's man, he doesn't believe in buying cut wood, since he could easily cut all the wood he needs himself, actually the very stove he warms his cabin with, better to fuel it with cut wood then to be dependent on gas or even electric, he can always cut more wood.

Retirement approaches and weeks before he sells the last of his working life's home, all the possessions in the city, so he and his loving wife can retire comfortably to the cabin at the lake. The woods and cabin have been calling him peaceably for as long as he can remember, how beautiful and relaxed is such a life.

On the morning of the first day of his retirement, our man's man goes down to the basement, as he has done so many times before, and puts some wood into the furnace to warm the house for the day. The wood was there already promptly stacked months before and comfortably waiting for the winter mornings that just started to appear.

He tries to climb out of the basement and stops at only the first step, because, he just can't catch his breath, finding for the first time in his life a lack of the strength he had so often just assumed would re-appear daily as he needed. He calls to his wife, who further calls paramedics and within a short moment, he finds himself being examined in the hospital by a team of doctors.

Cat scans, MRI, maybe they even do a biopsy or two, or not, and they go into the room to inform him and his awaiting wife that he has cancer. The doctors further inform him as to while they recommend chemo and radiation, the outlook does not look good and they think he only has months at best to live.

Our man, our hero, our professional football player, our brother, our husband, our father, dies that same day.

That man was told by someone he believed, trusted, for this man this doctor this learned-man must know true, and after hearing those words he had no doubt at all, he was going to die. He didn't want to die, why would he work so hard, so long to finally enjoy his earned retirement? No in his spirit he suddenly believed something and it happened.

No point in arguing, he died.

Today for the most part when we have an injury we are given something that will help reduce or remove the symptom we happen to be suffering from at that particular moment we are told what the expected outcome will be, then it is up to us to believe or not. Pills, always pills, always the ones the doctors say we need.

Steroids to reduce the bodies symptoms that actually are there to fight the issue at hand. Anti-inflammatory this, pain pills that, antibiotics, anti this, anti that. All these things designed to effectively reduce the irritations these infirmities cause, yet very few if any actually address in the least the actual cause of the issue and certainly does little to affect the mind or spirit at all.

So if we have already deduced that the spirit has the greatest portion of the whole, and the mind infinitely less, and the body really only has the smallest and most insignificant connection to the world, then we can assume that if using worldly means such as chemicals or physical applications it would only have the most insignificant effect on the healing process?

"The effective way to deal with any infirmity believe first in Me, see, hear, or experience something with the mind the Truth, and then act with the body move down that path."

PETER J COLLA

Storms of Life & The Bully

"Sicknesses, Injuries, Afflictions, or Infirmity's, are all storms, they blow in from afar, cause problems and fear, and in some cases damage even unto death, but for those who overcome the gift of each day is growth."

More and more I began to understand that afflictions seemed to come in waves, attacks or even in the form of storms, patients would almost without exception have the ability to pinpoint the actual moment they first became aware of an issue, whether it be a direct injury as in some kind of force injury such as a break or accident, or even when more slow progressing issues occur they could even with almost psychic clarity realize the very moment they first became aware that something was amiss?

"All infirmities whether sicknesses or injury all result from the same thing, they are the manifestation of storms that occur in peoples lives. Like storms a person must venture into them, whether by their own doing or carried on the back of others that ferry a soul through."

So you are saying many of the storms could be avoided?

"Of course. You chose the course especially after you are of the age of accountability. But once the storm is experienced it is up to you how you will deal with it, and this has a profound effect on how much if any damage occurs because of the storm."

There are many examples throughout history where people seem tool fall prey to sicknesses and the effects of the storms they feel with throughout the life they have set their own feet into, but yet others seem to go through the same storms unaffected, people are immune or just thought to be strong enough not to so-called catch the sickness others are seeming powerless to avoid, why is this?

I was often perplexed with the documented fact that people like Saint Francis of Assisi worked with and treated leapers yet never contracted the disease even though at the time there was no effective treatment or medicine for this severe affliction.

"Storms occur, there is nothing you can do except how you choose to deal with them?" *"Storms come upon you like a little child running into a bully."*

The Vision of the Bully and the little Girl;

To understand the nature of healing one must first examine and understand the aspects of exactly what is going on. A person cannot understand, let alone hope to fight a battle if they are looking in the wrong direction or blind to exactly what forces are attacking."

"Infirmities of all types, whether they be sicknesses, injuries, or afflictions that can last a lifetime, are attacks from the outside. People believed this once and today there needs to be a relearning of what is believed about such things."

Today People take their sicknesses upon themselves as if they are predesigned with or by some kind of mistake years before or worse yet a flaw in their genetic makeup. In days of past, we were told we came down with, afflicted by, or were tormented with this issue or that. Today were are being programmed by TV, doctors, and schools to believe we have it as if it is a part of us.

"Darkness can not make you into anything, I give you everything real in your life, but you do have the ability to created it in yourself, you have something when you believe

you do, confess it in your own life or accept what others have proclaimed unto you."

There are four examples I will use to describe the true nature of sicknesses as I have come to understand it to be in people s lives based on what I have witnessed over the years and what has been shown to me; "The Bully, the Raccoon, the Spy and the Hole in the Road".

Basically these are all the same but for the purpose of explanation and future reference we will use all four, and describe the nature of each of these attacks and then relate them to sicknesses or injuries in order to later reference them for further understanding of how to recognize them and what to do about them when they have already been defeated.

The Bully is a fine example of how sicknesses appear in the lives of ordinary innocent persons.

A child is walking to school and maybe has walked the same route over the course of weeks maybe even years, but every once in a while either they deviate from the path to a neighboring street or maybe take the not so frequented alleyway. Perhaps they are just meandering down the same street they have always ventured down. Along the way perhaps back from school, they suddenly come around the corner and walk right into the bully.

The bully frightens the child maybe even harasses or picks on the child, maybe dishes out a bruise, scratch, ache or pain or two, leaving the child venturing the rest of the way home, hurt, aching, crying, scared and feeling lonely.

Now if the parent is clueless, and not interested in getting any information from the child of why the abrasions suddenly appeared but merely picks up the child and bring them to the doctor, one might say that is still a good idea?

So the doctor examines the child, gives the mother some ointment for the abrasions, even advises the cautious parent to wash their hands before placing the ointment on the child's skin, because you wouldn't want to infect the child with germs that are resting on your own skin.

The doctor might even give the mother a pain pill to help with the pain, another to help with the tension or fear the child is suddenly suffering from, a nice full tube of oil-based antibacterial cream, cautioning the mother to keep an eye on the skin and if it shows increased signs of redness or irritation stop immediately with the cream, and while the doctor may be advised to the possible contra-indications such medicines have been known to facilitate, he does little if anything to warn about the various toxic chemical that the cream has in it. But at least he does warm the child not to put the cream anywhere near her mouth or eyes because it can cause severe irritation or even blindness. Yet with a satisfied customer and a collection of his deserved co-pay, he still prescribes the ointment for the bruises.

Now the child is not as enthusiastic when he doctor tells her she needs to stay home for at least a day or two, for she knows she will be behind in school, she already dreads what her teacher will say and certainly will need to make up the work.

Mother is told to put her in the room, get plenty of rest, and it might even be good to keep it dark to help her sleep.

The child leaves wondering about the dark room, needing to worry about the irritation of the ointment, the worry about just lying around in a dark room, thinking about the angry teacher and the extra work he will have to do, and most of all the worry about the trip back home the next time from school fearful the bully may come back.

Sickness is like the bully, it lays a thump on an innocent person, most of the time for being in the wrong place at the wrong time, and then goes its way leaving the undeserving child with the bruises, scrapes, and pains left over from the abuse. The bruises are not the bully, nor the ointment, but if the irritation was to spread because of the ointment, or the child was to suddenly develop a taste for the relief of the depression the pain pills seem to alleviate suddenly as she rests and the tension of going back to school suddenly is clouded by the drugs, one might easily confuse the ongoing issues with the ointment or the ongoing need to have pain pills as a continuation of the bullying.

As for true therapy to stop the cause, for the bully, once one understood where the bruises actually came from, of course, one could advise the child to not take that particular path. But also knowing where the attack might come from we were able to look out for the culprit, especially knowing with street they were hanging out and when they showed, a counter attack to fight back the bully might also be a good idea especially engaging the local law enforcement authority to ensure this behavior wasn't repeated with other innocents.

"This is a storm of angry malice. The disease is also not the bully but a spirit of malice driving the bully to do what he does"

"There are basically three ways you can deal with such a storm of malice; you can buckle down and take it, you can run and hide, or you can fight."

"Sicknesses, Infirmities, Injuries and Attacks, basically anything and everything that comes against you in the form of harming or hurtful to your life, does so always first in the form of a spiritual attack, these attacks must find an opening in your Temple and it is through this opening and only through this opening an attack can come."

"They might send in a lone attacker, attempting to do harm on the strength of an advisory, stabbing him or her in a place unsuspected whereby attempting to cripple them in their strength."

"Once the storm has arrived, and once you find yourself in the midst of it, dealing with the Storm, running no longer becomes a practical solution, leaving the remaining two options; just buckle down and take it, or fight."

Just Taking It

Just take it, seems to be the call sign of the general medical environment as we know it, whether it be by form of patient being told to "Take It!" being a pill, a dose of chemo, a recommended procedure that seems fruitless but needing to be done anyway, or merely the recommended direction and authorization being told to practitioners dished out with little or no explanation, and even less sympathy for the actual one needing help. People are being told to take something upon themselves, using the same word we might use or interpret to mean; "just allow it" because there is nothing you can do about it. Just like taking a beating from a bully, waiting in pain and fear until the blows subside.

Most injured people in my experience as a caregiver, general just take it, especially when it comes to dealing with afflictions or diseases. Some might say that taking penicillin or even choosing to exercise after getting an injury is a way of fighting back? But I have to say that as people get older they seem to more and more resolve themselves into the notion that these processes are inevitable and they are doomed to suffer these issues eventually, so the mere will to try to fight back even when it comes to simple choice of taking medications or exercising with therapy seems like an increasing lost cause.

"Your first mistake in that statement is people don't just get anything, they suffer from attacks from the outside, or worse yet open the gates of their own private temples. This is an open invitation to their bodies themselves, executed by their own actions, experiences, words, or very thoughts. More than any other way they precipitate the majority of attacks by the word preceding out of their own mouths."

"Jesus himself said; It is not what goes into the mouth but what precedeth out that corrupts a Man."

People often just take it, because they have either been convinced that they are powerless to do anything about it. Most of the time through misconceptions of the world and who they may have become, some misconceived notion of who they are destined to be, and in some more malevolent cases; because their own suffering actually profits the one doing the telling. Nowhere have I seen more examples of this than in the highest paid areas of health care.

The majority of the patients I have worked with over the years had a predisposed idea of the course of their illness or injury, and for the majority of them a simple resolution seemed to precipitate their expectations based initially upon whatever the doctor happen to tell them, but lately it was more based simply on something they read on the internet than anywhere else.

"Yes, individuals in authority lying to injured or suffering people for their own personal gains whether it be profit or simple evil wishing inwardly the child's utter detraction amounts to little more than vultures who feed upon the weak."

Also, I have found that people who didn't have this predisposed course of development or lack thereof would for the rest feel that they were getting exactly what they basically deserved because of some vivid action or habit they happen to practice years even decades before.

"Another lie whispered into innocent ears for the purpose of doubt and despair. Such whispers are perpetrated by the world designed for one purpose to convince My children that they were created less than the way I created them to be.

"You are all created perfect, remembered not forgotten, sought out and not abandoned, and most importantly forgiven with the sacrifice of My Own Son and never un-

forgiven. I Am a God that while giving every one of your life, have given you all the structures and support you will need to overcome all of the attacks you are meant to overcome."

"Suffering through, weathering the storm, lying down, and taking the beating, or settling for pain and death as a possible solution to just overcome, does not take faith but relies on doubt, doubt in Me for answers to the issues and attacks at hand."

As a medical provider I can honestly say that even back in my own education decades ago we were taught to instruct patients to blindly listen to our advice, trust only the accepted licensed medical providers of the specific areas, see everything outside the practice pharmaceutical insurance authorized mindset as hocus-pocus even to the point of if a solution wasn't possible when one doesn't exist.

"But for many, the idea of merely surviving has been perpetuated into the conscious of people, granting unto them posture that abandons Faith and takes on an attitude of voluntary enslavement."

"That is the battle for your soul."

Running Never Works

Bullies demonstrate themselves in many forms, not always limited to a pimple-faced somewhat overweight boy, large in stature for no other reason than the fact that at least one being held back in the early stages of his education experience, gave him the illusion that he was actually bigger than others. Lacking as much in the cute existential comment department as they do in compassion, but often present the heart that drives them to particular behaviors of cruelty perpetrated against weaker defenseless opponents, bullies present often times for reasons known only to their own jealous desires.

Once said bully is spotted, or at least finds himself within striking range, one of three responses for the would-be victim usually is eliminated especially if the Bully has already placed claws or filthy teeth on soft innocent flesh.

The first either, "Turn and Run," option is thwarted leaving only the "Just Take It?" or in some stronger and rarer cases "The Fight"? But we will further examine the run and hide option in part.

Turning represents a physical changing of direction from the path in which one has been set. When a person turns their back on something, it becomes difficult, if not impossible, to see it, thus the person turning to run becomes blind to everything that lies down that particular path they were on only moments before.

In the case of disease or other spontaneously occurring afflictions, many of these seem to arise without specific physical event tied to cause. But remember we are taught that diseases, which by the way we can never see because they are too small to see, to faint to smell, to light or few to feel, we just know or believe them to be real because we have been told.

But we are also programmed to feel we are absolutely helpless to these attacks, and the eventual destruction they might inflict, or at least we are told from our earliest memories. We don't see them, feel them or know for sure they are even present, but we are told, taught, and convinced they are real.

"Amazing how fear can make the most insignificant spec of essence into a giant."

"Avoiding the storm all together; which includes changing the direction you are walking through this journey which is your life, is not a bad idea, especially when the direction is wrong or destructive for you or others. Changing directions is not always feasible, considering some storms come up on people so fast and unexpected, it is almost impossible to avoid them."

I have noticed people who often avoid contact with infections at all cost or take extreme almost fanatic actions to isolate themselves from injuries, they end up wallowing in fear more than not and catch the very thing they fear.

"When a person does happen to see the danger and chooses a different path, leaves the previous experience or issue unresolved it will result into a constant searching the dark bushes and looking over the shoulder attack of fear, a distraction from the path immediately results. Take your eye off of where you are going or where exactly you are stepping and a fall is imminent."

"Fear that the bully or storm may show up along the new path taken. Fear is taken on by the child like a red cloak draped around the quivering shoulders in the middle of a field, and the angry bull is immediately attracted, resulting in the very thing the poor child fears."

"Both results are not the most desirable, and often result with the child having to suffer the brunt of the storm anyway."

No matter how a child tries to avoid or run, it seems like the bully always seems to find you and confrontation is inevitable.

"Yes with bullies and diseases the best is to stand your ground and fight."

"Do not fear, I am with you!"

I remember as a youth running and avoiding a bully for many months and possibly as much as a year until finally, I resolved myself I would not run again. Taking my normal route home I turned around some bushes along the path home just to find myself face to face with the bully.

A larger boy with a reputation for the cruelty he immediately started to advance but slowed when I held firm and said; "well I guess if we need to do this, we do?" Putting my hands up to defend myself.

Now I know the larger boy saw the fear in my eyes and his advance was certain, but the confidence quickly subsided as he looked past me at the figure who just stepped around the bushes after me. Ronny Mayberry an even larger more athletic boy from the same class suddenly steps from around the path and immediately moves towards the would be bully taking him firmly by the collar and stating in no uncertain terms that his bullying days were over.

While there wasn't much of size difference between them it was clear who was confident and now who was afraid. The would-be bully whimpered and made his promise and to my knowledge never bullied anyone again.

"Bullies like diseases are really cowards in disguise, turn on the light and they always run." "Ronny was an angel sent by me, he may have not even known it any more than the bully knew he was being used."

The essence of reality, funny how is it that people are so easily convinced what is reality and what is not, purely based on perspective, or experience, or even what others have told them. With medicine or in the case of sicknesses it is amazing how peoples symptoms will actually start matching the perspective symptom list of an injury even if these same people never demonstrated the original symptoms in the new areas, so strong is the mind and positive or in this case negative reinforcement.

The effect of negative reinforcement, where negative suggestions or images, sounds or ideas actually are reinforces by felt or imagined symptoms. This is nowhere more evident than in health care and the people claiming understanding and knowledge, doing the telling know nothing about the where these things come, what prompts or motivates them, where they are going, as a matter of fact, your entire medical health care temple with all of its potions and procedures cannot cure a single affliction or ailment, only God can.

As a matter of fact, it was a very disconcerting realization that with the exception of a few skilled individuals using techniques as old as civilizations themselves, repairing or even replacing damaged tissues with healthy undamaged replacements from others, very few procedures actually stimulate healing, but merely reduce symptoms of other injuries suffered earlier. I guess this all amounts to just taking it instead of actually fighting back.

So how do we actually fight?

"I will get to that in a minute, and yes fighting is the only solution; you are all called to be warriors and overcomer's in the battles of this life."

Turning one's back on the attacker puts them in a particularly vulnerable position, and by presenting one's back, it invites attack without defense, blind to any blows, tail tucked in pathetic attempt to protect private parts in the backside of running retreat.

Protecting private parts, now that's a statement; trying in some desperate way to protect a person's destiny, they which have not yet conceived in the future, even maybe their children, holding tightly to a hope that not only pain will be avoided, but perhaps other daybreaks warmth still might be found shining on their face, if only through survival.

I guess "Turning and Running" demonstrates and grants most assured defeat!

But let us make one thing clear, we are talking about a bully here, not standing and fighting battles we are not equipped, nor called to fight against in our proper time, by Him who would command us would for the most seem foolish.

"You should only fight the battles I call you to fight."

Running, and while in certain undeniable and overpowering attacks, survival can in itself finds certain qualities of victory, but for the sake of the bullying, we can assume that God will never place His children who seek Him in a place where defeat is possible, unless their time on the Earth has come to an end, as in the martyrs case, to be discussed later.

God has said in many places throughout the Bible; *"I will give you all you need!"*

"But my God shall supply all your need according to His riches in glory by Jesus Christ." Phil 4:19

"Seek ye first the kingdom of God, and His righteousness, and all things shall be given unto you." Matthew 6:33

Notice He says *"seek ye first"*, so by assumption, if we are seeking first, doing what we are supposed to, in each and every one of our steps, or at least when faced with such dilemmas, then we can also assume, by His promise, that He will give us all we need to overcome any challenge, any attack that presents itself on this path.

But God also doesn't honor the footsteps of fools. If we by our own selfish desires and sin find ourselves not only off the path but knee deep in the camp of the enemy, then getting everything we need to overcome, may just reside in a pair of good legs and enough oxygen in the blood, to get us out of there with barely our skin.

Back to the bully; running is defeat, and results in two things that only a good God could even remotely turn to positive; it reduces the value, the stature, of our, would-be hero in the eyes of most watching, those eyes of himself being the greatest affected. Popular phrases that one will often hear include; "Once a coward always a coward", "You chicken", or "Scattering of the roaches" these just being a few terms, that have been associated with people who flee. Gods ability to even turn this into positive is without dispute, for no other reason then just because He said so, but we will have to reserve this topic for future writing.

The second effect of running is that it builds the confidence of said bully. Making it more likely he will just do his mouthing-off again, louder next time, more often, and cause even more damage in the direct vicinity. So confident is the bully of where he has been that he doesn't even look back. And why should he, only the conquered reside behind him? But it is in his confidence that he exposes his weakness.

"Look to me and you will be given the answers you seek."

PETER J COLLA

Stand and Fight

"The final choice, the best choice; Stand and fight".

"Standing and Fighting" grants and demonstrates certain victorious parts! Victory is victory!

By definition first a person must stand; get up, rise, now with this image carries a meaning of an immediate and direct increase in stature. When a person rises to the occasion, they grow larger, and in direct counter, their opponent will decrease, if by no other means then just simple vantage point. As a person being attacked gets higher, the object against which one stands appears smaller.

To stand also implies to find firm foundation, one can only successfully achieve firm foundation if they press against something also firm, rock being the strongest, but make no mistake even a deep foundation in sand, the key being deep, can be a significant pillar for resistance. God describes studying the Word as finding deep foundation or building on the rock, both apply.

As I have already stated the physical changes that one will

benefit from in standing and fighting, those being first an increase of the defender, and a decrease of the attacker. These are immediate and Godly provisions given by the natural laws that nobody can deny. There is movement and that movement is backward into a realm the giant never looks, he has no experience there.

But let us examine further some supernatural effects, those under the skin.

What must have gone through Goliath's mind, and maybe even that dark hole which represents his heart, when David walked out there unto the battle plain? And we might even possibly take a glance at what may have been going on supernaturally, in and around the environment.

First, In Goliath's experience everyone who had ever faced him ran, only the poor unfortunate's that he may have been chased down, fought back in some kind of pathetic defense as he dished out his cruel blows. For an oversized opponent, forward motion has it's advantages. Forward momentum of any type is a force that must be resisted, held in check, overcome, and eventually overpowered in order to turn an attacker into a retreating posture. Very difficult situation when facing something that big, no maybe the largest warrior to ever step up.

So when Goliath saw someone step up and faced him, even just a boy moving towards him rather than away, most likely doubt from witnessing something new and yet unseen must have at least tickled the edges of his senses. It wasn't tickling the hordes in the supernatural, for the wave of force that shot through their ranks most assuredly shook them to their black bones.

He was bigger than anyone, so fighting from a height advantage in downward blows, allowed him to engage much stronger muscle groups then having to fight upward. Goliath was used to only forward motion, using his imposing size, weight, and great strength to do most of his work for him.

When David stood, the increased advantage, even if it had been but a slight decreasing effect on Goliath, it was a decrease none-the-less! Anyone who participates in any kind of top sport activity will tell you momentum is a powerful thing, and when someone starts downward, or decreasing in trend, that it is usually coupled with some kind loss and or pain.

Next David not only took Goliath's insults and threats, but laughed at them and responded with his own, backed by the power of the Creator of the Universe!

Oops!

Suddenly Goliath's words that usually made his opponents quiver made this person laugh, but notice Goliath wasn't laughing, he was to busy shaking from the Lion's roar he just heard! Something was seriously wrong here for Goliath and for the first time in his life he might have even felt that cold chill go up his spine, and if he wasn't, he should have been!

Momentum shifting, from Goliath moving forward his whole life, to being suddenly held in check, someone stepping up, him shrinking in stature, and getting less then expected result from his threats, even resulting in further diminishing on the bullies part. Momentum had shifted!

Goliath threw out a desperate comment, trying to weaken David with statements of; "You come at me like a dog, with a stick." His comment was not as much of a joke, but a feeble attack, for it was designed to make David believe he is ill equipped to the task.

But David's faith and the trust he had everything he would need from God to defeat this man, threw the insult right back stating that Goliath's weapons were nothing compared to that of the Living God. And if Goliath's eyes weren't wide with fear at the power of these words, they where the moment the giant took but a single step forward and David started running straight towards him!

At every turn victory was accomplished, and the actual deliverance had not even been dealt out yet. In everyone's eyes, natural and in the supernatural, there was no doubt as to the sudden cease and immediate reversal of the momentum.

I can imagine on the barren plain of the supernatural where a horde of demonic legions stood moving comfortably forward against the children of God, riding on the backside of Goliath's image, the attack's and effect's of the constant bombardment of fear, doubt, hopelessness, rejection, abandonment, as well as doom, must have been nearly overpowering to the soldiers of God's army.

Many a troop probably were gripped in such paralyzing oppression that they were to busy protecting their soft underbellies in some kind of fetal self comfort, to even pick up the sword and shield that lied only a hands reach from them. I can hardly imagine the refreshing warmth that must have flowed over them like anointing oil as the demon horde immediately stopped the attack, withdrawing into their own defensive positioning at the sign of the sudden and direct momentum shift exploding in front of them like a nuclear explosion of bright holy light!

Thousands of smaller demons squealed and ran almost immediately as the light went on! "A Scattering of the Roaches" does apply here very nicely! There must have also been an immediate withdrawing of the more herd animal type troops, first pulling back hard and then interlocking the shields in some kind of desperate counter defensive. This had no doubt, sent that physical twinge up the spine of not only Goliath, but all of the Philistine troops assembled, cold and lonely was its chill. A direct opposite the counter anointing, the refreshing warmth that must have thrust power and confidence into the souls and bodies of the Israeli army.

But I also know when David charged, any demons of herd animal status, the entire front lines, dropped everything and ran, even trampling those who were not as fortunate to get out of the way. That's what herd animals do when someone charges. Ripples of fear and fiery Godly retribution sent choking shivers through the remaining demonic soldiers, and this feeling was backed by the power and presence of the God who created the universe.

The Stone, the hurdling of the rock, the spoken

manifestation, the small representation of the word of God, even in it's simplest form, was all it took to open the floodgates of Gods deliverance. David could have thrown anything, the giant was already doomed, but throwing out a single small piece of the Word was all it took.

Once contact was made the result was immediate and sealed. Down onto his face Goliath fell, back exposed, demons of all ranks were running for their lives, very much emulated in the natural as the armies of the Philistine who also broke ranks and ran.

At this point all that remained was the mopping up! David casually walks up and takes Goliath's head, his victory prize to present to the king. The armies of the Living God pursue now in frenzied strength, I am sure empowered by the angelic horde that wraps themselves in and around all of the arms and souls of the Lord's army until all of the opposing force has been hunted down and killed. The Bible speaks of bodies being scattered across the country side. It took a little time, and effort, but victory was granted long before the army was destroyed.

A woman sits comfortably in her home, a child of the Living God, she closes her eyes in quiet contemplation of the path that God has placed her two beautiful feet on. As she strides up the path, eyes focused on the radiating light shining out from the destination her soul draws to, led in quiet solitude by the spirit that grows within in each and every step, she is only just beginning to feel the pestering pull of the voices on the few strings that remain within her house.

On a hill a horde is forming, gathered to distract even if only her eye from task. They are not trying to pull her from the path, that is not their job, but they do belong to the army of he who feels he can, given the right positioning, preparation, and infiltration. But for now the task at hand is distraction, keep the door open, keep that earthly ash blowing into her house if, for no other reasons then to dirty up the corners.

God gives her this day a vision, and in this vision she sees, no maybe just feels, the spirit that rests within cigarettes, it is a worm! It startles her, and she throws the cigarette down, almost an immediate reaction to discovering the creature. Worms, foul creatures that sneak in the most indiscriminate way, finding access inside the temple, then uses it's own hunger and greed to burrow inside feeding on the blessings of God, unknown, hidden, until it has done so much damage that rot and sickness is assured.

But in the vision also she throws it down!!! Momentum!

"Wait!" she says, she pleads for council, help, she turns to God....She walks up to the battle field, she stands!

This time she stands. She has someone with her, another trying to help her, encourage her, endear her with courage!

One of the commanders among the demonic horde screams with the top of his dirty longs; "How dare anyone tell me I shouldn't smoke!" "It's my right!" The voice is a confident one, a giant, a veteran of many battles.

Anger presses from its words, if only by their forward momentum, insult follows, feelings of insufficiency, inadequacy, doubt drips like black blood off the spear tips of a "right to do what I want." But the resistance this time is met with a different power, the power of love and light; she stands, firm in the word, deep in its foundation, and dead in their tracks the front lines of the demon horde stops almost causing the lines to crash into itself! They take up defensive position.

Their insult's and attack's do some hit home, doubt's and fear's find open window's in the house, chink's in the armor but the posture of the woman continues to stand further and further erect. The fear and chill ripples through the attacking group now frozen in fear, they even try to take cautious and unbelievable steps backward if just to find their own firm footing, but they have none but muck and mud.

Her words; "I want this to be gone from me", "I don't want this in my life any more", "help me", send out their own volleys of the word, the difference hers is backed with the power of a living God, speaking of a child calling to a Father for help.

She is tired, she is a child, voicing if only calls of pain and weakness in standing alone; "I've tried and always failed in the past", but these are also call's to the Father for His help.

"Lord I believe, now help me with my unbelief"

And she actually starts running at them!! She moves towards them in a real and physical attack of her own, she go's to get an unused cigarette to "throw it down". For as she saw in the vision, she is about to duplicate in the real physical.

Words of encouragement ring in her ear;

"Pick up your matt and walk!" How must that have sounded to the man who was crippled his whole life. For just a moment, do you think something dark may have whispered

into his ear; "What is he crazy, you can't, you tried so many times"? Maybe he even reached up for help, but God gave him all he needed to overcome, and he stood?

How long after, maybe every time after he walked, and stepped just this way or that, did a feeling, a twinge in his newly healed legs, brought back a voice the enemy whispers; "Its back, you see, temporary, you weren't really healed,"

The continuing of believing, that is called work.

The Bible tells us in John 9: 13-34, of a blind man who was cured by Jesus, and when he presented himself to the priests they tried to discredit Jesus, thus discrediting the mans healing itself, but he refused to buckle. The man stood on faith, even unto pressure, fear, ridicule, for himself, and his parents who also had been held, he held to the healing in faith, and many times confessed with his mouth; "For before I was blind, and now I can see", "if This Man where not of God, He could do nothing."

On the barren plain, fear of the pure power of the Living God exploded through the demonic horde as fast as a blast of irradiated light of the greatest flash ever witnessed. The front line buckles and explodes in a moment. From a barrier and confidence that has been no doubt built over years, toppled in a moment. As the demonic troop scatters, a wall of dark black brick is clearly seen, most likely that of which these creatures have been leaning against, hiding, almost secretly building inside the courtyard of God's beautiful child for years.

She takes a hand full of the arrows, yet unused, some that have yet to hit their intended mark, and she throws them down in a thunderous explosion. "From the ground you come and into the ground you shall go again!"

The ripple of the power sends a shock wave through the ground like a massive earthquake wave right into the enemies camp, and like a vast wave rolling through a calm still black lake, so confident they were in their hold and position there wasn't even a ripple on their surface of their darks waters, until now.

As the wave explodes through the dark waters, it becomes clear and sure to see, not deep were their murky secrets, an illusion of lies and discrete. The wave gathers strength as it approaches the wall, it seems to be powered by her momentum, and that of the Word, exploding into the dark wall sending it toppling like a flimsy card house of black dominoes.

Face down in the muck lies the one that yelled; "How dare you tell me I can't smoke, it's my right!"

The worm faced giant lay face down in the muck, back exposed waiting only for deaths victory to be dealt out.

She stamps them mercilessly into the ground, for they showed her no mercy as they tried to steal her gifts.

Time to mop up! She stamps the cigarettes into the ground in defiance.

Yes, there are groups of fleeing troops that have run to the trees, waiting for some reinforcements for small counter attacks. Waiting for orders, they still turn and fling arrows of doubt. Tossing accusations against those who helped her, doubt, challenges to her to turn and run, more doubt, calling to her "if you doubt any you must doubt all", trying to shake even her faith that God could or would help her, more doubt, but her shield is up and deflection is becoming something she is beginning to master. One by one each of these little attacks fall, time, distance, and perseverance must follow to mop up the entire army.

Victory is undeniable! The stronghold has been toppled! Now the mess has to be cleaned up, many dirty bricks lay around, held together with the mortar of ash. The black ash water is just settling, the clear water pressing the ash into the soil soon to become the fertilizer of another beautiful patch of garden. Her house, her lands are called to be a garden, not a barren plain of ash.

Yes, there will be skirmishes, troops will attack, some she may lose, but many she will win, and ever will their numbers slowly dissipate until the last of the retreating horde finds itself defeated or banished.

So is it.

"Supernatural battles against sickness such as that of Michelle all look similar to this one, turn on the light and darkness flees."

Raccoons In the House

"The Raccoon story is a great example I gave you to how people let sicknesses in themselves and they usually suffer the consequences after unaware of an attack has even happened."

"What do you know about Raccoons?"

The first step in confronting and eventually eliminating any medical issue a person may be suffering from on an ongoing basis resides in the identification of the irritant, it is first necessary to understand the issue at hand and exactly what we are fighting.

Given the fact that we are the greatest proportion of our essence is spirit then we must also realize that anything that happens to us good or bad in our lives is primarily spirit based, and knowing this makes it so much easier to fight and defeat in the case of a negative confrontation.

We have been taught we have little or no influence on the outcomes of issues that afflict us, that we are some sort of random occurrence and when bad things happen to us it is just Karma, bad luck, or being at the wrong place at the wrong time. But this misconception has the effect of taking the Divine out of our paths and makes us a bit of a slave to whatever infirmity that may present itself. It is so easy with such thought to just give up and not even begin to hope when we are suddenly deceived into believing we are afflicted with a dreadful occurrence.

If we will further suppose that all injuries of any type are a result of attacks, then like any of these attacks, there is a specific direction from which it comes, there is a weakness in our own personal defenses that this attack and others like it may have breached, and if we can identify exactly what direction and in what manner the attack is occurring, we can use this information to fight back!

"You can only effectively fight an attacking hoard if you are facing them when they attack. In war, information is key to victory."

I can remember with not such fond recollection living up in the forest and deciding one day to take the kids on a picnic for the evening. We made a whole bunch of baked chicken, packed up all the supplies and headed off to the lake many miles away.

What I didn't realize was we left one of the containers of the chicken out on the counter cooling. There were a few, so missing one was not noticeable. Neither did the boys notice the window they left open earlier that day. We didn't notice anything until we got home late that night and saw that the house had been ransacked, the cushions were destroyed, everything had been toppled over, and the place looked and smelled like a garbage bomb went off! We had been living in this home, in the forest for years and never had such an attack before. Amazing what a couple of little raccoons could do.

Anyone who might on an occasion or two had the privilege of running into a close encounter with raccoons might have a story quite similar to this one.

This particular raccoon story manifested as it were in the home that I enjoyed out in the middle of the forest, unaware and ill-prepared for the mess that was about to come.

One summer weekend we decided to spend the afternoon at the lake, going through the usual preparations, buying and packing all the necessary food and entertainment materials we would need for the day.

The kids would pack the things they might need or use, and we would prepare the food in advance, making it easier to just have fun and not have to worry about bringing all the cooking supplies a longer and more complex dinner preparation might require. In this particular trip, three trays of chicken were on the menu, three trays to be exact, all of which was prepared grilled to cooked perfection beforehand.

The chicken, three trays cooled on the counter, for we were having all of the extended family join us as well, and the baskets were filled and packed for the lunch and evening feast. All the materials were placed in the various picnic baskets we brought, and as soon as the truck was loaded we were off.

It wasn't until the evening dinner that we realized that we had left one of the three trays of chicken behind. Not a devastating problem for we had prepared extra and had plenty of the other food to feed everyone. Campfire and the customary evening fun, pack up a bit later and go home.

As we opened the door of the home we realized the place was in shambles, mess everywhere, couches were torn up, garbage, chicken bones and stink all over the floors. The mess, damage, and feces were everywhere, and suddenly I heard a sound coming from the boy's bedroom. I immediately started making a loud noise to scare them away just in case it was a bear?

We quickly turned on the light and grabbed the shotgun heading cautiously down the hall towards the room, for one still wasn't sure what we were dealing with, but "bear" being a real possibility, and until we actually laid eyes on it we needed to be careful.

A small scampering noise coming from the boys' room? But unfortunately, or perhaps, fortunately, the creatures escaped out of the window in the boy's room before I entered. There were clearly dirty animal tracks up the wall and out the open window; Raccoons!

My son was wide-eyed, and a bit scares as he realized he had left the window open that morning. He left the window open, I left the bait in the form of the chicken, the raccoons accepted the invitation and decided to show up and have a party.

"The raccoon attack is as sicknesses, the mess is what happens when it stays awhile unnoticed."

Therapy; now the first thing we did was turn on the light! Yes, that had the effect of scaring away the animals, maybe they just heard our talking, even our voices screaming for whatever is in the house to get out, but most likely they wanted to just get away seemingly undetected since they were obviously full having accomplished what they came for; chicken dinner!

But low and behold the damage was done, the house was in shambles and some of the destruction may not even be able to be repaired depending on the extent of the damage done.

"This storm and the winds of menacing raccoons is a perfect example of sicknesses and the effects they have on the body."

The next step was close the window! If we had not realized that animals were even there and merely assumed maybe the house was burglarized or even more absurd; an earthquake or a tornado inside the house may have done this, or even more idiotic, that the house was somehow defective and this mess was a part of what it was?

One may have not made the connection of the window and the attack and after clean up efforts were complete, everyone went to bed, the now newly hungered raccoons may have returned to perform another examination of the refrigerator or perhaps the trash this time.

Silly how if people never realize they have a raccoon infestation, or a problem leaving windows open and food out on the counter, one might begin to think they are just unlucky or have a bad house prone to strange and sudden spontaneous garbage explosions from out of the garbage bin.

But if our pioneers of the rugged forest are clever enough to realize they not only left the window open but may have even baited the animals in, closing off these two factors quickly reduces the chances for reoccurrence and leaves them with step three of the true rehabilitation; mopping up the mess.

"People sit and take it thinking the mess or the bruises are the sicknesses while the actual malevolent attack has long gone, or worse they sit in their house unaware continuing to inflict damage."

So like the raccoons we must identify the issues and then look for them, turn on the lights, get loud and they will just run off?

"Yes, like the raccoons in the story the first moment you become aware an attack has occurred or you are in the process of an attack you must first, turn on the Light, then tell it to leave."

"I am the Light"

"Look to Me first and then the answers will be given."

"Most have not because they ask not."

"After this pick up the weapons I have given you, and if need be drive them out."

It is amazing but when you look at the healing Jesus demonstrated and see them not only through body, mind and spiritual perspective but also from a health care practitioners perspective it is clear He gave so many examples of this. As a matter of fact, He gave us a complete and thorough program of how you should rid ourselves of all these afflictions.

The Spirit of God brought all the necessary specific examples to his followers so they could write them down, in a way that completely documents everything each of us needs to free themselves of any and all afflictions.

"Jesus healed millions of people, in the short span of His actual teaching life, as a matter of fact, he healed in one way or another every single person He came in contact with. For it was written, if they had written down every miracle He had performed it would fill all the books ever written in the world."

"I didn't need to bombard you with endless repetition of miracle after miracle, only teach you of the significant ones that describe how not only you must identify God in everything around you, but see the spiritual side of sicknesses if you truly want to combat them thoroughly and effectively from every perspective you are afflicted."

PETER J COLLA

Fear Not

"Choose not to fear, it is a choice."

Fear is the greatest cause of dilapidation in human existence. It is quite clear and now commonly known that people can even die from fear.

The mind has enormous influence on the body, and when the mind gets overwhelmed with pain signals it is completely possible for a person to die without any clear physical termination of function. Prior to the development of modern anesthetic, people would often die before the operation or procedures could progress even the point of being life-threatening themselves merely because a person was experiencing such severe pain.

But belief, or what people believe, influences strongly the mind and the interpretation of not only the sensations we feel but what they mean to our well being, future and prospects of fulfilling the dreams of yesterday. Patients will often come in with a predisposed idea of how a process will unfold actually looking for manifested symptoms that qualify those outlooks even before they actually show up. Basically, they believe themselves into becoming sick.

These ideas or ideologies about expected symptoms will often also cause them to become fixated on the issues at hand disregarding everything else revolving around them. This mindset, in essence, concentrates their attention on the smallest structures in their body placing an almost giant like image on the smallest structure in their body but also placing them into a posture of submission to this smallest irritant and allow it to completely take over their lives. They fear pain and the afflictions of what might happen to them.

I would say pain is the enemies greatest weapon.

"No, pain is not of the enemy, pain is the warning system I have built into you to give you warning of an attack, from what direction, and exactly what is being attacked, even what door or window the attack is trying to use, what path it is trying to impair."

"*Fear does this to people, it causes you to focus on what is not, taking your mind off all of the rest of what you have. Fear is the enemies and sicknesses greatest weapon.*"

"*He says Fear Not more than anything else, but never say do not have pain. Pain is information, listen to what it is telling you immediately, and act positively and it will stop. Once the fire alarm is responded to and action is taken, it is no longer needing to ring.*"

"*Spy's are like unto sicknesses, they often sneak in almost unobservable ways, just to wreak havoc in their malevolent assignments dwelling in darkness hidden until their presence is actually discovered, it is only then that they are either chased off or captured and destroyed.*"

"*Sicknesses are like spies, they are so small and insignificant in their creation, almost like insects, like the scorpion, it is quiet and for the most part docile but when it gets activated by agitation it becomes crazy on the attack, yes it will even go into such a frenzy causing often a risk of its own life, for in the scorpion the anger overwhelms it with foolishness.*"

The larger the creature, the harder and more pinpoint the attack plan must be.

Jesus showed even this, In some cases, demons can only be freed from their attacking hosts through prayer and fasting. Fasting is one of the greatest tools you can use for activating heavenly reactions to earthly issues.

The reality of the spy! In war and even in peace, a spy can infiltrate a social circle and through the infliction of damage or theft, can place a balanced and successful social structure suddenly in turmoil. From the outside and with the wrong information, people might believe as the structures or functions suddenly begin to dissimilate the problem merely lies in a spontaneous breakdown of normal function common with a complex working structure.

When subsequent repairs are performed and the same structures or other related ones suddenly follow the perplexing result in a sort of cat chasing its own tail scenario developing whereby people may throw water on the fire but if a person doesn't address the fare starter more fires will just irrupt.

The good news is as in the case of the spy, merely realizing that there may be an outside agent or spy, inflicting these attacks, will have the profound result of chasing first the spy off and then when subsequent repairs occur there is no repeated destruction or continual disruption occurring.

Spy's, like cockroaches, or the most basic animals, know when they are being hunted, they are the most basic of creations, and while they may be cunning they are also cowards and no stomach for direct confrontation, regardless of how many James Bonds' may speak to the contrary.

"So what exactly happens when we suddenly put the light on and the cockroach is spotted, he runs like crazy. Sickness is every bit the same."

"You know you are under attack, first turn on the light."

PETER J COLLA

Turn on the Light

When I first began to examine the possibility that a more supernatural occurrence may be in play in the area of healing, I placed into me as a practitioner in an immediate and almost perplexing notion; "Why do some people get healed and others seem to not?"

I have seen it played out time and time again, whereby people with seemingly the exact issues and the exact condition, one will recover and sometimes even in miraculous manners, while others seem to have their issue continue with seemingly no long-term elevation, no matter what is done?

With first glance the issue could be attested to age or condition of the person being treated, perhaps it is pre-disposition or their nutritional habits, maybe it is other habits that hinder or stimulate such rapid recoveries or lack thereof? But the more I seemed to delve into studying the patterns of recovery and the greater the cases quantities that were examined the sooner I realized that no set factors or relative principles could be determined that would attest to one specific advantage or not other than the obvious age-related advantages, and even then often would from time to time present also anomalies that defied explanation; such as young children who would not recover even with seemingly minimal pertinent afflictions, while some elderly also would almost miraculously recover with only the simplest and brief interventions.

I immediately began to examine various aspects of healing and how they related to manifested aspects of what people related to almost miraculous healing. Examining aspects of prayer and what effect this had on patients knowing or even unknowingly engaged. Various aspects of natural medicines were increasingly used in the therapeutic venue also to attempt to see if by inclusion any of these or possibly all of them may lead to increased effectiveness of the treatment regiments already considered.

In essence, I was searching for the key to discover what I referred too and I may understand as the "God Gene". It was a blind adventure that lasted months even years, as various aspects of the natural were presented, tried and tabulated always adding these procedures into the already present model.

The result; when I added anything that was natural, good, loving or Godly, people would have positive results, many instantaneous and completely unexpected. But I found that with many the results didn't last. People would return days, weeks or even moments later with a return of the same symptoms.

"That is because you were only treating a fraction of the person, touching upon the symptoms, great or small, these are only a small fraction of the actual story that represents every person that presents themselves to you."

"If you want to fix a broken house, and all you do is fill a single crack on the wall with a little plaster and paint, you are doomed to not only have a very small success rate, you are actually guilty of inadvertently being paid for nothing."

I not so quickly realized that if you want to heal people with a large amount of success you must treat the whole person, thus examine the entire person. But what was the exact person? We are more than just bodies, feet, knees, backs, ligaments, muscles, skin, systems, blood, brains, hearts or pieces. We are more than just minds, with experiences past present and even dreamed about in the future. We are more than just beliefs with every emotion, hope, love, desire, hate aspiration and fear. We are an accumulation of all of these things.

So knowing this, how does a person who wants to effectively help another person heal and desires to effect this healing on all levels as to increase the effectiveness of said treatment how does a person examine the issues on all these levels simultaneously?

I had no idea so I asked.

"You start by turning on the light."

"Turning on the light is nothing more than asking God what is going on?"

"You have not because you ask not. And ask anything in my name and I will grant you even more than I had done on earth because I am in heaven with my father."

"Promises!"

"Step one Ask God. Turn on the light, lift your head, just like with Michelle, call out and whatever God reveals, act on it."

"Just being willing to look in the direction of God is the first act of faith."

I immediately went on a program during examination to have people not only tell me what happened physically to them when they first felt the injury or affliction, but what exactly were they busy within their minds at the time of the attack and more importantly what were they struggling within their belief systems what was pulling at them in their lives.

The injury almost every time mimicked in the location of attack issues they were struggling within their life.

People with great issues of carrying burdens in their life compounded issues in their back. People who were having issues deciding which direction to go would develop neck problems, shoulders for issues of great mobility or lack thereof in their current situations.

Heart problems for people struggling with family issues or decisions they had made that affected their families. Intestinal problems with people having a hard time letting go of the past issues, weight problems when they would stuff emotionally, cancer when battles would rage within them.

Anxiety with unresolved fears, balance when the confusion of their life became unbearable and unresolvable. Lung problems with people who had issues with speech, eye problems when they knew they were looking in the wrong places. On and on the similarities emerged and frankly what was amazing was that in every case when people were willing to examining there might be a spiritual meaning to the even or attack in their life they almost always and completely knew exactly what and why it was happening to them and the organs or extremities involved.

"Exactly, after you turn on the light the next step is to just simply and quietly ask why?"

"Why this issue, at this time, in this place on my body? What are you supposed to learn from this experience, remember what doesn't kill you makes you stronger?"

God can turn all things to good for those who seek Him.

"What are you supposed to learn at the moment of the attack, what are you to overcome? How are you better, stronger, wiser, it is at this moment of asking the lights come on and the darkness must flee."

The Still Soft Voice

"The very moment you feel the attack, whatever the feeling is, if it is something out of the ordinary and you feel it is negative intention against you, that is the moment of the infirmities attack and you turn the light on by becoming aware of what it really is; tell it to leave."

"You will do all the things you see me do and greater because I am with my Father in heaven. Just believe. I have given you authority over those dark spirits."

I can say that every patient that I spoke to regardless of the disease, injury, or process knew the very moment they started feeling something wasn't right and it usually started with a little irritation or a simple pain, cough, dizziness, anxiety, cramp, stiffness, numbness, some kind of irritant that felt out of the ordinary, enough to bring their attention to it.

So why not just tell something to leave, or for that matter "command" the issue to leave? I began to talk to the people about what I was attempting myself in treatment, even going so far to ask if they felt anything different, and then describe it, or to outright tell them I was in a sense praying for them when I was laying my hands on them.

The reception was for the most part much nicer and well received then I had expected. Over the course of my education, the teaching community would almost with fanatic zeal infused into the minds of its students the need to clearly and emphatically keep the ideas of God or any kind of religion out of the medical treatment arena. There was almost a sort of "Separation of Church and State" attitude placed into the health care education basis, we practitioners being the state, and while it wasn't exactly forbidden, a sense of if you did pray for your patients, don't let them know, or certainly don't tell the Doctors, unless you wanted to blackballed as a heretic or something.

But the people themselves, in most cases, seemed to actually be thankful for your intention to actually ask God to help them or at least a deep desire to give them something more than just the cold and unfeeling application of another treatment. Often commenting about the treatments they had received prior feeling like some cold dead pill, non-feeling and heartless merely ushering them in and out of the office like cattle.

They received words of hope and prayer even if in the most meager sense often with open hands and hearts eager like children to see what good thing this unexpected treat might bring? So I began to apply it in the most rudimentary sense, surrounding the patients with imagery and sounds that for the most part spoke of peace, goodness, faith, love, and freedom. The effect on the treatment outcomes was astonishing, I began to see immediate results and heard reports of people experiencing immediate improvements some before any physical procedure occurred.

I began to find a greater and more concentrated effect when words were associated with the treatment application. Thus when I would express in words what I attempted to display in touch, and then gave the expected outcome in a sort of positive reinforcement, the effect was almost always tightened, consistent and seemed to be more long-lasting.

But what about when the damage had already been done?

"So ok, now here we sit, the bug bites you on the leg and leaves, what now?"

Healing like wisdom rains down all of the children constantly and continually like the random droplet falling on the parched dry ground of a summers desert day, we people decide two things; first whether or not to actually take the gift as it rains down and then what exactly to do with it.

"First thing you need to do is ensure you don't keep getting bitten over and over again. One must make sure they don't continue to revisit the place, that caused them the injury in the first place."

"You all walk through gardens of life, stepping stones that waver along a path of your own choosing. Often stepping off the path even for a moment to enjoy the creation along the way whether be it laying in the grass, or partaking of a flower that you happen to glance as you walk. These actions of creations all have effects on the universe around you because in essence you create events forever realized and as ripples through still waters these events have effects good

and bad on the surrounding universe you constantly re-created."

How often have I seen in the course of my career people leaving the office with the necessary information they need to overcome, sometimes even with a complete alleviation of symptoms relating to the injury all together, just to return a day or two later with the exact returning injury, or to return only a few months later with a similar injury. Many cases knowing exactly what situation precipitated the issue in the first place, but then go right back to action or place in their life where the issue occurred just to have it happen again.

"This happens because people first don't see the injury as a product of their occurrence in time, or a test to produce a new and renewed victory, merely a result of bad luck. It is this mentality that has had an effect on the whole, basically taking the miraculous out of healing and perpetuating an increasing ideology of fear."

People seem to have this return to the bowl that caused the issue in the first place mentality. I guess changing lifestyles is among the most difficult things anyone can do.

"It is the purpose of the model of today's Western medicine to perpetuate fear, and it's this stepping away from Faith that actually not only leads to attracting more attacks but leads to voluntary enslavement of life's posture."

"The worst is that fear perpetuates a realization of the very thing people fear, especially when they continually voice, or speak this thing into reality with their very own words."

Sounds like the power of positive attraction, positive reinforcement, or positive thinking?

"Those like so many gifts I have rained down on all My children are only a piece of the creation, if you want to understand and apply them to the whole then you must examine the whole and consider it completely. If you receive a gift from God such as healing, peace, love, or faith then you must recognize where it comes from otherwise the gift becomes veiled in the pride and desires of the earth."

"In essence it where you store your treasures you receive. You can store them on earth where there is rust, worms, and thieves, or you can store them in heaven where there is no rust, no worm to eat, no thief to steal."

The positive words have such an influence on the outcomes of the treatments especially the effects. Many people will come in and ask; "can you help take away my pain?" Not realizing that in the same sentence in which they ask for the issue to be removed, they also claim it as their own.

"I Am is the greatest single power in the universe, for it is a manifested confession of God Himself."

"When you claim to be someone such as this kind of patient or that, giving yourself, or even accepting labels others place upon you, it is at that moment you basically become what you command."

I noticed over the course of my thirty years of a career in healthcare a sort of shift in how things were realized especially in the media, among my colleagues, and it may have even been how things were subtly taught in schools.

Earlier I can remember stating that people were afflicted with this or that, and even came down with a particular injury or sickness, now people for the most state they "have" something or they are this sickness or that.

"That shifting in belief is a dark and diabolical lie designed enslave My people in their afflictions and present them powerless and in chains to the malevolent dark spirits that wish to destroy their souls."

That is so true especially in the health care area, I noticed when people began to believe they have become something, while they may wish for their symptoms to be alleviated, they had not the slightest fraction of hope to think they could be cured. They were already told by doctors there was no cure, the sickness was permanent, terminal, there was nothing that could be done about it, whether it was the doctor telling them, the TV, or even something they read on the internet, they believed it.

Calling yourself a diabetic instead of saying; I am suffering from diabetes is the same as giving up on fighting and just taking it without a fight. What about all the other labels?

"You are what you claim you are. Anything less than a child of God is an insult."

Labels have become the mainstay and as I look back it was almost as subtle as a snake the way it progressed through the medical society and field of medicine as a whole. First, there was the formulation of diagnosis codes, whereby a number would be placed on a person identifying them with a particular sickness that people through symptom identification would be suffering from.

No care, prescription, healthcare benefit, or authorization would be granted without the corresponding diagnosis code being placed upon a patient. Then once the code was given the corresponding treatment could not be deviated from regardless of the personal aspects or symptoms a particular person might demonstrate. Patients, in essence, became the what they were labeled.

They became amputees instead of suffering from an injury that resulted in an amputation. They became migraine patients instead of suffering from a migraine. They became total knee patients, total hips, stroke patients, cancer patients, all of the issues that seemed earlier merely to be products of something else.

People stopped believing they were suffering from addictions and started believing they were addicts, obese, had high blood pressure, are depressed rather than suffering from depression, that they are disabled!

There are no more patients, there are no more terminally ill, only God has the right to determine when a person shall live or die, and only God who creates every day new decides how each of us are to live. We get to decide what we want to look at whether it be the life, light, and everything good in our day or the what we don't have the shadows the negative, the labels placed on us by darkness.

When people stop seeing it as something they are being afflicted with, but something they have become, they, in essence, stop seeing themselves as overcomer's, bowing down in submission and just take it. This is what must stop.

"You are not created to be slaves, but to become Kings and Queens."

Words have power, it begins with people letting go of the labels, people need to change their thinking about themselves even if it merely with words. Some of the first therapeutic procedures would be having the people do was only refer to themselves with good, uplifting or positive words, and notice I didn't say "patients", because I started telling people not to refer to themselves as patients any longer.

When they speak of the symptoms they happen to be suffering from, do just that speak of them as if the symptoms are something afflicting them from outside themselves because they are? Even though the pain might be inside a person, pain is merely a signal that something else is occurring, it is that which needs to stop!

"First, turn on the light, then speak the truth."

PETER J COLLA

Why the Leg

There is more to the story here. Why the leg?

If it is all a challenge, a task, an opportunity to overcome and grow, and if the Father can turn all things to good, then we must have a reason why the leg? The legs propel us through this life, so an attack against the legs is an attack against the very journey we find ourselves on.

So, people who have injuries to their legs, this is an attempt to challenge their journey?

"Sometimes, yes, sometimes they are on the wrong path, or merely find themselves walking in the wrong direction, but sometimes they are on the right path and the challenge is designed to stop them. Only each individual can come to know, and then, if they chose, overcome, that is once they come to the age of accountability."

So what about children, what happens when they are attacked with injuries or sicknesses?

"Children are so often the intended victims of malevolent attacks, but how they react is not up to them but their parents, doctors, teachers, coaches, and other people who have been given responsibility for these innocents. In the majority of afflictions, it is the parent who needs the treatment, through the parent the child overcomes."

"A sickness can be fed to a child one spoonful at a time as easy as telling the same child they are sick or are something less than how they were created to be, and that is perfect."

I have personally treated children who were born with Palsy from birth, and it is difficult to see perfection in such drastic injuries?

"You are still looking at my children through the veils of the world, not everyone is born with every blessing of the garden, the poor will always be with you, but every soul is perfect when it is created, they chose light or dark each in their own time, free will."

"I would that you all come to me as children, accepting the truth as the truth, unveiled and free of the shadows of earthly doubt."

Attacks against the body are storms designed to change the course of your soul through the gardens God has destined each of us individually to walk. The "why" is always present in the attack, given to us as signs to show everyone the information as to what we may learn from these experiences. This is perhaps what God meant when He said; "Be of good cheer when you are persecuted...," because knowing we will come out better and stronger can to a degree give one comfort when the pain, storm, or anguish is upon us.

In the case of legs, people who may be destined to travel great distances and do great things with the product of their steps, the enemy can't know their future nor even the essentials of what exactly this path means, it merely sees in the supernatural a talent in the area of journey expressed in the product of manifestation that presents itself as strong legs supernaturally. So he attacks the legs as a hope to first stop the ability to journey and perhaps destroy a persons' soul their very dreams causing them to despair and give up.

How can we know if we are being attacked or on the wrong path?

Since these challenges and injuries are always attacks, we merely must go back to the source and try to surmise the essence of what is happening, where you came from and where you are going to understand if the chosen path truly is the one. Seek knowledge from the very source of Creation, one must stop, rest, meditate or pray, and understand. If we are on a path that we know to be good and true, then the only assumption we can make is that its an attempt to stop us.

"You will know when you are at peace. People have a distinct understanding even genuine knowing of when they are going in the right direction and when they are not. If you are ever in doubt all you have to do is ask the One who truly is interested in your happiness."

This makes so much sense. A person who has strong legs spiritually and is destined to go to great places, might be attacked in the knees stop this motion, and at the very least has the effect of placing fear in the mind of this person in the future, stopping them from pursuing a purpose of course of their life that might involve a great deal of motion of the legs. One attack left unresolved puts fear in every thought regarding movement or travel, and thus the person allows fear to be an open window in their spiritual house in which attacking spirits can constantly revisit throughout their lives.

It is no wonder why many people will have one issue resolved may be operated on such as a ruptured disc in the back, just to have other later seemingly out of the blue rupture, without any trauma even close to the original injury.

"Leave the window open the raccoons just come back later."

"Wisdom is the greatest thing you can ask for, no more so than in healing. Ask and ye shall receive!"

"You were created to lie down in green pastures and lay beside still waters, remember? This means basically this world was created for you to rest and enjoy without strife and in peace, but unfortunately, men have re-created a world where this has become increasingly more difficult to realize."

PETER J COLLA

Speak It Into Reality

So the first exercise or thing that must happen in the therapeutic process of injury recovery is a vocal manifestation of what we are expecting. Believe it has become manifested even in word, act upon it, and then witness the increase in our life in response. Any progress is progress!

People have a trouble understanding that each and every moment of life is a gift, and as such there is truly something perfect and godly to experience even in a single breath, but it is the worries and troubles of the world, its responsibilities and pondering that has robbed people of the gifts they could experience if they just stopped and saw them.

I myself have been so guilty of these worries and anxieties whether they be pain, problems, storms, tragedies, whatever, they always have the effect of taking my eyes off the world around me and placing them on the very small, and often yet to materialize, worry I happen to be dwelling on at that moment.

The solution is an active and conscious decision not to look at negative, shadows, or worry but look up and out into the world around to see the light of the gift God has given right at this moment.

Did He not say; *"Go your faith has made you whole."*

When it comes to people suffering from injury the instruction becomes one of reinforced positive experience on every point of experience possible, basically sight, sound, taste, and smell, even feeling. Feel the soft touch of the loving partners' caress and realize the pain has gone. Inject good into any situation and it becomes better!

So by vocalizing the healing, that we have been promised the victory is received, the actual creation in our spoken voice puts into place the positive motion of the reality created.

So often as it is seen in the common medical community, people have become fearful of the unseen and cruel sicknesses that seem to lurk in the shadows of their lives. These pour souls then contract a simple symptom such as a bite, a harsh touch, or inkling of rebellion in their body, at which time their minds immediately go to the worst-case scenario. They speak negativity into and with their words, their every thought, and in fear go to the doctors who are quick to label it, label them, search for it, test for it, pray to God that "It" hasn't already become what they already are claiming with their many words, thoughts, and fears.

These poor victims may feel a twinge in their chest or pain in their head, somewhere along the way they left a door open inter-house or stepped into a hole and a little creature bit them.

Doubt turns into fear, fear into self-cursing, ultimately they draw the curse themselves like a wild animal-drawn to a fearful rabbit under a tree, or worse yet, others speak it at them. Fear is the catnip of the spiritual world.

They go to people who they trust to tell them the answers, people who have been given authority to know the answers.

Unfortunately, these very people they go to are the same ones taught by the industries, philosophies, or spirits that want all of us to put our trust not in God, but in oil-based drugs or practices of darkness. These same practices only seem to enslave us, fill us with doubt, or lead us onto a road of depression, poverty and ultimately death.

One after another these poor individuals are given drugs and instructed, or pressed upon, or in some cases as in innocents forced upon them, to put every foul sort of toxin of the world in their mouths in a feeble attempt to try to elevate some initial symptom. This symptom being nothing more than an alarm bell to warn us of an issue or cause, so unaffected by the drug we are taking, that these same causes maybe even in some cases could be precipitated or even enhanced by the same said drug,

"I give them everything they need to overcome every obstacle this life might seem to place in their way."

What does this mean? We are given in this life each and every day we open our eyes all the things we need to overcome the challenges of that day? Perhaps it means we have already been given everything in this life we may need to overcome any physical infirmity at hand, we merely have to reach out and use it.

"Both! That is exactly what it means."

People think that life, especially the body is everything, then the mind controls the body actions and events, a little less, and finally, the spirit is the least significant part floating somewhere apart or on your shoulder whispering softly in your ear. That being said medicines which have a dramatic effect on the body must be the solution for issues of the body?

Yes, that would be true if you were but flesh, but we are more than flesh, we are more than minds, and as we have already seen we are primarily and for the most part spirits. Spirits while being slightly influenced by earthly poisons, are only in the most fractional basis influenced by the physical poisons of a single day. No different than dropping a drop of poison into the sea, what effect does it really have on the whole?

"Spirit attacks spirit!"

"They hate my children so, not the germs, not the foolish vessels that think that what they are doing is actually helping them, yet has the most long-lasting effect on their own lives. Not the foolish scorpions being used to their own destruction, no the spirits that drive them, that is the enemy."

Back to healing, in life, as in health and wellness people have basically two choices; they can be persons dancing through the beautiful garden of life looking at every beautiful flower in their garden as they head towards the light, or they can sit in the dirt staring at their little toe wondering in oblivion why it hurts even though the just watched the scorpion run away or cower in the corner like the coward it is.

"When you are a person who looks to God for life and every stone in which to step as you pass through your own garden which is your soul, you have absolutely nothing to fear because I am with you."

"My rod and staff will comfort you."

So if we see or know of a bully down a particular street and choose to take another path, we must not fear. I have noticed through my own experiences that on occasion I might find myself on the wrong path or direction in life and suddenly I am at times granted a brief but somewhat fearful warning like the hair-raising in the back of my head?

"Yes, this is my messenger or an angel gently warning you of impending dangers or attacks. For those who are listening to Me, not being completely distracted by complications or the misguided necessities of the world around them, these gentle nudges or signs come daily as people quickly run through the fields of my glorious creation for them each and every day."

"Here again look up, and speak into your life the reality of what you want."

Back to the best way people should deal with sicknesses, so what should a person do about if they happen to been bitten?

We have already realized that lifting up the head and after turning on the light, there is a promised realization of the truth, this seeking the wisdom, asking for help, represents an active and positive choice to seek light in a persons life and facilitates them immediately upon the road to healing. What next?

"Put on the full armor of God. Next, pick up the tools to defend yourself, I provide the rod and staff, you can call to angels for help, turning on the bright light is a battle plan, creatures of the night always run away from bright light."

The world has made people afraid of light, with all the UV scare and everything, getting themselves to cover up completely, hide in the dark, stick their head in the sand, most of the time looking to something good, natural, or simply seems to be the opposite of what is instructed especially in medicine. I have even over the last couple of years seen more and more examples of people being prescribed chemotherapies or other extremely dangerous treatment methods even when no cancer or other harmful issues have been detected, and in some cases merely as a preventative measure just in case.

"Water is the best and most abundant physical component for healing, any therapeutic process or mopping up should use water."

Be a fireman, turn on the water and direct it, a good water hose can scare any animal away much more effectively than any gun.

"Water is a good start."

PETER J COLLA

Overcoming

If we suppose that everything in this creation is at hand for us to use for the overcoming of any issue people face then you must believe; "Everything You Need" means everything, and every issue not only means the hole, the wolf, the disease, cancer, whatever, but also the effects of the fall!

"I create all of my children, every single day, with everything they need to overcome every issue they will need throughout that particular day in their life. As a matter of fact, I create them with everything they need in every single breath!"

I have heard that statement before "Life in every breath" from my own martial arts training, but isn't that a Buddhist thought having to do with the search for balance, war, and peace, training the fighting skills and balancing them with painting, dance, or poetry, various art practices to create harmony?

"I rain my wisdom down on all my children heads indiscreetly as a way to show them all my creation. Nothing I share with you is more or different than anything I have shared with everyone else, the only difference is you chose to listen, write it down and share it with others."

Older patients even mention family traits or things that they did in the past that basically pre-destine them into suffering from issues but I have seen when people apply the principles as spoken of earlier then use all natural and God-given elements to facilitate the clean up of the mess almost miraculous healing and even a sort of turning back of the clock restoration occurs.

People are deceived into thinking they are doomed because of the mistakes or abuses of the past, the same way they are also deceived by the misconception that there is nothing they can do about their issue themselves but must look to a more learned and regulated industry to secure any kind of assurance or insurance of health. This goes in direct contradiction to the promise that Christ made us during his time on earth and documented by His examples.

"Overcoming amounts to nothing more than simply stepping up onto the water and walking above the waves in a storm."

For the first time in History people were healed, blind people regained their sight, the dead rose, people of all sorts of afflictions were suddenly or systematically healed. These were documented events that nobody disputes, many of such cases find themselves common occurrences today, I have even personally spoken to many people who have sprung back to life some as a result of medical interventions, others in a few cases even came back with no medical intervention at all, merely because they were told to on the other side.

But nowhere have I ever heard of anyone walking on water.

"When you take control of a storm in your belief, understanding the image, waves, and winds have no effect on you unless you let them, in essence, you step up above the waves and walk on the water."

"All storms no matter what you call them, sickness, disease, addiction, depression, all forms of attacks are all the same

merely movements of energies surrounding you and being directed to attack you. Now that you know how insignificant the spiritual energies that direct them are compared to you and the powers I have granted you, stepping out above them is as simple as lifting your head."

Stepping over the attacks is one thing, then choosing what tools will need to be used for the cleaning up or restorations caused by the damage already perpetrated by the storm is another. People still suffer from the aftermath of the bug bite, no matter how small. I knew a man I loved, a dear friend, a good man, who lost a leg because of a bug bite.

"When the attack occurs and leaves a child with a mess to clean up, use anything and everything I give you right at hand to continue to overcome and move further through your garden."

I began to instruct the people who came to me to only use natural products as much as they can. Use water in every aspect of the therapeutic process, whether it be baths, pools, wet compresses, or simple flushing with water. When water could not be confirmed to be clean, do the best a person could to filter it and when in doubt bless it.

"Water is my conduit to relay emotions such as love, faith, and belief, I am the living waters, and if you bless them with your own love they will manifest love where ever and in whatever fashion you use them."

Using all forms of goodness in every portal in our being assures us that light is being applied in every door entering our life, it is the most absolute avenue to ensure success. Good natural light, looking only at good peaceful images when seeking healing and therapeutic responses from our bodies. Treatments in nature or in a garden become much more beneficial than the sterile typical treatment office where all natural light is closed off.

This is the single most advantageous application therapy for treating children regardless of their afflictions. I was amazed that when these factors would be applied to children more then anyone demonstrated the most rapid and seemingly miraculous ability to overcome and heal.

"I would that all of you come to me as children."

Good peaceful sounds such as calming music or soft meditation music aids in the sound department when granting a positive environment for healing, but filling the ears with nothing negative, only positive uplifting and encouraging words is key for the increase of goodness in one's life. And if success is to be guaranteed then words of forgiveness spoken and heard are instrumental for driving away spirits that may still be inflicting a person.

But remember always forgive yourself for being a participant in the issues that have harmed you. People themselves are always their own hardest judges, forgiving others for the very things they refuse to forgive themselves for.

Good natural foods, pure natural plant products for the reduction of symptoms, natural oils for positive applications of love and care in massages, touches and natural reflex treatments any and all of these are just a few of everything that resides around us merely to be picked up and used for the treatment of issues arising from the survival of a storm.

"A loving touch is a gift you can so freely give, and its treasure is beyond your ability to totally comprehend in the physical   world."

Touch My People

When given the question, and wondering about a possibility of healing someone, almost from the first moment of awareness people associate the thought of healing with the sense of touch, being that which people need to initiate in order to facilitate the healing.

If we consider the natural world and look carefully, it his almost immediately clear with each and every injury a person responds almost naturally and immediately to touch.

A Mothers' child hurt themselves and the mother almost instinctively takes the child and kisses the hurt, caresses them, or holds them in a comforting manner, embellishing love, giving compassion and fulfilling comfort. The child receives this and immediately responds, there is an immediate calming of irritation, a relaxing of tension and a realization that everything will be all right.

Science would say the stimulation of fine touch nerves overwhelms the slower pain receiving nerves and the pain is not felt as the child receive comforting stimulus instead of pain, but I would like to also believe the child receives love in the way of warmth transmitted in real perceivable energy by the mother in the form of caring emotional love being given through her concern, love, and compassion. This the child feels this deep within, and experiences as not only a superficial warming sensation on the skin but a penetrating radiating feeling of love that perpetually courses through to the bone. A belief is expressed and generated in the form of love, life, peace and joy, and all these feeling overpower the recent feelings of destruction, pain, fear, and sadness.

"Inject love and the darkness immediately flees."

I decide to put this to the test and began to see if the people could actually feel when I was truly was expressing a feeling of concern, and wondered if they were aware of such feelings at all, especially if unexpressed by me. The only thing I could think of was asking within myself was a simple prayer as I laid my hands on them.

While I was not in my opinion one who considered himself a praying individual, a simple; "Please help this person" seemed all I needed and the concentration of wanting the person to feel the warmth of this statement as I played my hand on them even for the most simple massaging technique, seemed to be sufficient to elicit an immediate and palatable response from the person being treated.

I was amazed at the reactions of the people, they almost always immediately became aware that my hands became warmer and even in many cases hot, feeling a sort of deep heating experience much deeper and more pronounced than they had ever felt before, especially aware of this sensation since I had started treating them?

But what now, did the people when they felt this warmth, did they heal? Many often felt better, some significantly better, even to the point to where the pain or irritation would simply disappear, but often and is many cases the pain would only reappear later or the next day, and the person would come back for another of the same experience of relief. This left me with only more questions, what is the purpose of this revelation, and how could it be used in the process of helping heal people?

"Warmth you felt in your hands and so many others who have had a calling into the healing arena is a gift, a sign that they are engaging in a path of righteousness. Everyone who has been healed is called then in their own turn to help heal others, this is how the healing gene is engaged and mobilized."

I have over the course of my years of practice heard of and even met many who have received this gift of "healing hands", some have been hailed as healers, but many the gift was not sustainable, working for some and not for others, this too is a perplexing issue to consider, especially when these same people later come to light as being perpetrators of hoaxes or fraud merely as a means to extort sums of money from believing and gullible crowd.

"My blessing rain down on all my children heads like raindrops being scattered in the winds, regardless of the boundaries, whether they be countries, races, or even religions. Men place these boundaries on each other attributing some qualifiers as if my love needs a qualifier. If I have given life to any of the children of the world would I not rain down blessing also indiscriminately?"

"It is when these individuals have received one or more blessings, such as the honor of being used by Me to heal another individual, and then take this honor upon themselves somehow believing that the healing powers comes from them instead of Me, it at the moment they have elevated themselves above God and then I remove the ability for them to command the action, for they command in their own name and not mine."

"They either become blinded by the veils of the world or remain blind in their own journeys far off the paths of light and life I would create for them."

"Unfortunately for many, they fall victim of vanity, finding the need to regurgitate the healing event for a paying audience. This is a slander against God, and the spirits that drive vanity, greed, and lust for power, have one goal of their own existence, and that is to be seen, lure followers away from God and destroy the gifts of God."

I have experience practitioners of true or God-centered faith when receiving the healing gift, whether being healed themselves or students of healing instructions experience a true desire to be a part of this experience at least in their own desire to support the experience in others. There seems to be an overwhelming desire to share what they have received.

"Healing is like unto sowing of the seed, and when this then comes on to harvest will grow, multiply and become bountiful even unto feeding many others."

"The evidence of this is a continuation of their own examination of creation, people who seek light, goodness, and healing for others, seek all of these things for themselves."

"Light draws the light, and for all who seek truth, goodness, love, peace, if they look far enough and remove the veils from their eyes of man-made prodigiousness, they will find Me calling them."

"That is why one must always remember where true healing comes from, and give credit, where credit is due."

"You have heard a simple explanation of what sickness is, healing is just as simple."

PETER J COLLA

Fasting is Good

"Fasting is an amplifier for intensifying your prayers, need answers fast."

"Want healing, direction, actions from above, fast! For whatever you do, do it as of unto Me and I will give it right back to you. Give, and it shall be given unto you; good measure, pressed down, and shaken together, and running over."

"Fasting beats down the body so that you can feel and even hear the spirit."

I have recently begun to advise anyone wishing to make health and wellness a real part of their life, at least when it comes to seeking advice in their physical therapy health, adding fasting to their program has not only benefits but truly limitless almost infinite positive attributes that dwarf even the most powerful chemical medications.

Food is truly one of Gods blessings and when the same Godly respect is made towards the feast, only Godly results seem to come.

"Breaking of bread, what could be so delicious?"

The aroma meanders through the chamber like a soft cool summers breeze, dancing on the edge of the senses with the soft-footed gentleness of the most beautiful young princess, whisking of flowing light garments. It touches the inner senses with a deep sense of satisfaction, feeding the hunger of body's pure delight. It's very bouquet has the amazing ability to both satisfy and illicit further hunger.

A golden loaf of light browns and earthly tans, crusted flakes, out from the warmth that bursts from within. Light goes in, binds to the essence of the pure white grain that rests under the surface, wrapping its arms around the bread that will not only give but sustain life. Heat, warm light, God's created gift of being presented to the body for the nourishing of its parts, given by God for all parts equally, needed and free with love.

There is just a singe on the bottom where the bread came in contact with the fire baked stones, heat, and fire to erupt the life-generating processes that expand this wonderful gift of God from mere elements of the earth. Life within life, grain, yeast, water, a touch of salt, and oil, all the gifts of whom any a part might need.

He broke the bread gave it to his disciples and said; *"Take this, all of you and eat of it, for this is my body, my body which has been given for you."*

"Take this and eat, in remembrance of me."

The bread was broken and given to all, everyone present took a piece, receiving all they needed, all that could be given by the bread.

Even as the foot sits in the dust, and has not the privilege to hear bread's crispy sound as the loaf is broken, does the foot not benefit equally as the ear?

And as the hand which can feel the warmth, and has the privilege to break it, and give it, will never see its beautiful golden color, does the hand experience less?

The mouth can taste this wonderful blessing, and even to the One who speaks those Words, also tastes the same sweet flavors, as all that recline at the table. What gift does Father have for Him, the Son, does He not receive likewise an equal gift from the Father?

They all hear the Words, created by the Father; Son, sinner, and saint, all equally given, even as the rain falls on everyone's head.

Even as the One gave, takes He also a taste, for as God gives so, does He feed in the pleasure of the gift.

Being raised a Catholic, the act of taking communion was taught to be something of reverence, a moment of sanctification.

But as I have spoken of the experience with others; a common question seems to speak through peoples heart, lingering on quivering lips as if an unspoken secret, a dark question one might hardly dare think, let alone speak; "I don't know, but have you ever felt anything significant during the act of communion"?

Resting in the depths of such a question, there resides a feeling of doubt, guilt for some kind of lack thereof, as if belief might somehow be substantiated by the very manifest of such a question. How many souls have doubted their own beliefs as a result of the un-appearance of an emotional connection to communion?

There are many churches out there, in addition, where the taking of communion is only allowed if a number of prerequisite tasks are first completed. Rules need to be obeyed, people are told they must be or become members, given permission, a class or two might need to be taken, a prerequisite kneeling before a man, or just by being someone who happens to be appropriately dressed, and or employed. Oh, and heaven forbid if they have participated in any activities that the said church deems unforgivable, prior to wishing to participate?

I have even heard them go so far as to say; if people partake without meeting the prerequisite set of qualifiers, they even risk a dire punishment from God, even unto death.

Well, I felt God prompting me to examine this for a moment.

There seems to be a number of examples of an instance in which Jesus sits and dines, or drinks with people, in any and all of these instances, I have never heard him once place any kind of admission prerequisite in any of these attendances. As a matter of fact, in most cases He seemed to sit and dine with not only tax collectors and prostitutes, considered in that time to be the absolute bottom of society not only in cleanliness, but undeniably in the eyes of the church government at the time, but did He also not sit with the Pharisees and Sadducees who Jesus himself referred to as *"A Den of Vipers"*.

Or resting casually on the side of a perfect green grass carpeted hill as a few loaves and fishes are broken and given all to everyone over five thousand present, to the point of giving complete nourishment, with an abundant overfull, leaving nobody unnourished, who would but partake.

Either way in both cases there seems to be no prerequisite prompting to do anything prior to eating or drinking.

Yes, He did say; *"Do this in memory of me,"* when He shared His last breaking of bread and drank with them.

But why "Think of Him" with this act?

Why not "Think of Me before you sleep" or "every time you kiss someone you love"? And while I believe there may be many reasons for the significance of breaking bread and drinking of a cup, as infinite many as there are infinite images of the Face of God all around us, one, in particular, comes to mind to this writer;

If God would have us think of Him, as often as we could, even with every waking breath, what a good start would it be for His children to at least think of Him and the sacrifice He made for each of us, with something that we at least do each and every day; eat and drink.

Some people need a physical representation of a supernatural act in order to bring heaven to earth in their mind.

A real feel of something in their hand, so as to give the blessing to the hand.

Something to the lips, as to bless the lips and even more the mouth taking in the taste and reality of the gift.

Something to the ear, hearing the Word and through the sound, a creation of an image in our mind, not all that different than the creation of the entire universe by a single spoken Work back at the beginning of existence.

But did Jesus place any prerequisite as to who he shared bread with, who might hear, who might see? The invitation to the table, and as glorious as it must have been, there is no apparent sound of any word of restriction or exclusion. And while nobody was sent away, one did leave, turned and ran from the presence of God.

And even Jesus himself warned; *"Better it is that one was never born than to betray the Son of Man"*, for sacrificed was but the reason He came to the earth.

For it is clearly written in Luke 22: 17-20 He shared bread and cup in the last supper, asking them to remember Him.

And it wasn't until the next moment Luke 22: 21 that Jesus states; "But, Behold, the hand of him who betrayeth me is with me on the table".

It was further written that "the darkness came into him" because at that point Judas made his choice, and he fled. *"For darkness looked upon light and it comprehended it not, and darkness fled."*

Sharing at the table of the Lord, while one partakes of a piece, all share, all are welcome.

As they take all from the same loaf, so is a piece of the same given to each, and each as a part of the whole enjoys and benefit's in maybe a slightly different manner, but all are fed, all receive nourishment.

The Word that is given to a man through a man,

Who is God,

But has become Man,

As to reach us all,

In loving gesture to come home.

A request to choose,

Not a command to bow,

But merely to request to remember,

The sacrifice the Prince gave each and every one of us.

That Word which is Him,

But is also part of a one as it passes through him,

And as a part,

It is of Him if but for a moment,

Becoming Him the Word,

Resting on the edge of his tongue and soul.

The thought which is God,

Granted in His wisdom's gift,

Is life created out of light,

Baked with the fire of glory,

And resonates into existence,

For all the ears to hear.

In the ears of all that come,

The Word rests on the surface of His children,

All who would hear,

God touching the ear of each,

And forming a picture,

Creating in the mind of each of their soul's.

The eyes then take each image in,

Each and every gift of The Fathers creation,

Every color forming into beautiful picture,

Blending with their luscious desires,

Fulfilling the hunger and pains as it forms in the mind,

That loneliness that has lingered since birth's first day.

Grant to each of us,

In every part,

All that we would but need,

In our every part,

Each in its capacity to feel, all what you would give.

Every hand that takes the bread,

Every eye that takes the gift in,

With the ears receiving of Word,

With the mouth sweet taste,

In to the body for all parts to benefit.

Is it not with any word given to any part of the body, any prophesy, any healing, can they not be used for all of the body?

Is not every gift for the body, if it is given by God for the entire body, all to use all equal all free?

"Dear Lord Jesus, help me to think of You each and every time I but eat or drink, for as freely as I receive the gift of these life-giving nourishment, You gave Your sacrifice for my salvation as well. I merely have to believe and remember this simple fact, to receive the washing of my soul and clear out any darkness, so when I look at You, The Light, I will not flee, receiving the healing you have so freely given and paid for with your blood."

PETER J COLLA

False god, a Glimpse

Ok, let us get right into it!

Mitra is the pagan god of insurance or the assurance of health and welfare to all that will worship it. It has transcended through the ages, mimicking Jesus in every way it can, as almost every high voluted demonic pagan self-proclaimed god did, being the so-called benevolence of kindness. Claiming to be of a virgin birth or pure. Claiming the same date of birth as our Savior. Even sending out twelve teachers as its emissaries to teach it's horse piled lies. It is a true Anti-Christ, something that promises what Christ freely gives, but delivers the opposite. Claims to be of the light, but is filled to the brim with darkness.

Amazing how all these false gods want the same thing; control, first fruits, and our ultimate destruction.

In the early kingdoms of Mesopotamia, Egypt, Babylon, Rome, just to name a few, Mitra, a figure of a woman, adorned in golden jewelry, was worshiped by laying gold, or the first fruits of one's labors at her feet, for the assurance of getting through the next years harvest. Insurance against destruction, a promise, give her your first fruits now and she will take care of you in the time of need. Sounds familiar?

Does it surprise anyone, that Mitra was on the symbol, or used by the initial founding companies for the life insurance that later turned into the health insurance companies of today? Look it up!

Most insurance companies have no problem writing a check to deliver death and darkness into the vein through chemo, paying upwards of $10,000 per inter-veinous chemotherapy treatment, or paying for an abortion. But to ask them to pay for a woman to have an early preventative mamma-gram, than the averages or computer screen says, even after she feels a small lump, forget it! Or an extra visit for a man trying to rehabilitate his back so he can return to work and support his family, no way.

You want the truth; I have seen it all; demographic denial approval based purely on where in town people lives, authorizing care then sending denials to the patient to scare them into quitting, bumping up patient responsibility or co-pays up until the point where the so-called co-pay represents almost the entire bill, purposed losing of information merely to stall approval, waiting until the period of care is exhausted then making the approval knowing full well the care can no longer take place in the specified time frame, even claim reps throwing claims in the garbage.

Another common trick is hiring secondary management companies that deny everything, and then the insurance company itself doesn't even have to take the blame for the denial. And on and on it goes, tricks after tricks designed for one thing; to steal more from the people in what was promised a paid in advance benefit, while they hold the gold in the fat coffins of the money changers that call themselves the insurance companies.

If all gifts come from God, then so did the knowledge that was given to our fathers and mothers in the form of advances in health care. And while Doctors should be paid an honest fee for their services, companies have no right delving out those gifts given to our fathers at such exorbitant fees or costs, that it would put a family into lifetime ruination merely to perform a service that saves a child or wife's life.

A doctor has a gift, of this no one doubts, and they should be paid for their gift according to supply and demand. They should have the right to set those prices of their care, not insurance companies or their cloned servants the hospitals, and let the doctor look into the face of the child he is treating to see if his own eyes can live with the price he places on that service.

And what is wrong with a system that through government mandate forces participation. Forcing people to participate in a system that in itself demands them to bow down and give homage to a spiritual entity.

And what about the Doctors? Why should they be forced to perform surgeries in places that are so exaggerated in costs by the insurance companies, that a mere days stay costs the patient $10,000? While at the same time paying back to the insurance company malpractice insurance fees (a mandatory fee, often in the $100,000 or more range per year), as well as fees for participation (contracting fees) with the insurance companies themselves. If there was a fair price paid to people who were the victim of malpractice, perhaps the doctors wouldn't need to be scared into believing they have to pay such exorbitant fees just to survive such a lawsuit.

What are we to do? Trust again in God, for by Who only through Him healing comes. Turn away from the dependency of insurance spirit, and call for true health care reform; a return to a fair price for a fair product, putting an end to a few using those gifts God given our fathers; treatments for the aiding in the healing of children, and share again that which people need for all at a fair price. A return to a fair price for a fair product even in hospitals, where they are held accountable for costs, kept fair and demonstrated that are not in the business of stealing.

And instead of paying billions to the democracy of health care, a fool website that doesn't work, or agencies sole purpose is to cut cost at the expense of care, use those monies for the people whose costs are greater than can be paid under normal circumstance.

Look to the days of the country Doctor, when almost every form of care was given at the office, a simple remedy or tea was enough to solve most ailments, instead of some oil based pill that while it helps with one symptom causes five others. And the cost, well if you didn't have the money, for the most part, a chicken or baby pig, or quilted blanket, or a heartfelt thank you was enough.

"Dear Jesus let us not fall prey to the greed and traps of dark spirits, free us from the fear that has been spoken into our ears through servants of evil. Let us remember He, You Lord Jesus, and through You, all healing comes only from the Father, help us trust, and thus give glory where and to Whom the glory is due."

PETER J COLLA

Cleaning Out Cobwebs In My Soul

"Saul (Paul) why do you persecute me?"

I found myself retreating more and more to the mountains, for some it is the sea, others a quiet trek along a natural trail perhaps a trusted companion in the form of a dog walking eagerly at your side, a garden bench, or even solitary room to just go and find yourself at peace away and perhaps engulfed in the pure creation of the new day.

For me, Pagosa Springs had quickly become my place where I could sit and listen for answers. On one particular day, I sat among a group of young brothers and sisters in this beautiful mountain town of Pagosa Springs, find myself waiting patiently, even hoping for the Lord to descend on this meager band. I say young, being from ages of mere adults to seventy-plus years on this earth. I guess if we consider, we will all have an endless millennium to yet live, even a seventy or so lifespan would be but a blink in the totality of what is to come.

First of all, does He descend, as so many of us eager believers have been led to understand by a church who presents to us the interpretation of His Word, or is He ever-present?

I believe the latter, as any good Father would do, sometimes just keeping his face barely out of our immediate sight, for one purpose, and one alone, to promote our growth. As to when He does show up, in a more experiential way; one. He will manifest His presence in a real way, especially when we present ourselves as much as we can in a pure and unblemished sacrifice to Him, or two, He just shows up whenever He feels like it, as to benefit the Kingdom.

The long weekend had been a mixed bag of mountaintop experiences, mostly finding us serving the needs of various peoples longing to taste a bite of the feast that we have been so privileged to dine, healing and God-given health being the subject of discussion more often than not. When I say serve, each of us rests in, better yet takes upon themselves, the privilege of service. How sweet is the taste of service for the Kingdom, especially when you are in the service of the King, and not only yourself?

Splintered off into various fractions of the whole group, each in his turn being drawn into the conversations of which weaves the fabric of the lives of those who have come to visit.

As guests come, these interactions propel us into a realm of His word, commissioning's occur; assignments are handed to officers in His End Times Army, healing's descending from above; not all clearly seen in the physical, but undeniable realized in mind, heart, or combining-ly the soul. Wisdom gets poured out like cool clear water from the sweet vessels of children who again obediently submit, what is clearly amazing is who are the ones learning, that fact is not always exactly clear.

As I think back throughout the weekend, and examine with more from a distant view, it is clear to me that preparations were all made not by us, but from above, and as such, in each of us as participants, the only prerequisite was "a willingness to obey, and to show up."

First, a man obeys, makes the trip, submits and puts down any and all cloaks of pride allowing the Holy Spirit to work a cleansing stroke through his soul. What is missing, for some reason something seems to be?

Then there is a listening stage, in which the toughest part is pushing out the deep routed desires to sleep, and grasp an idea that even as we see people in need around us, there is a possibility that these people are being presented in front of us as to show the possibility of the same need in ourselves.

This is the essence of giving up the cloak of pride, because if we listen through the veils of our own church wisdom, we might actually hear the very Words the Holy Spirit will deliver to us individually, there might be a new message, something new to see, a revelation, in each and every experience we have witnessed throughout the day.

"Every person you have ever treated also was a teacher for you. Every interaction between two spirits is an exchange of energy, love, light, and healing. You think you are bringing healing, it is you receiving healing as well."

We all were being transformed through reflection, words, some understood some not so, teachings, visions, prayer, acts of giving, opportunities to heal and be healed. Not as much of a change, as a final cleaning up of the rooms that had been built by the seeds of those present only moments before this wonderful coming together occurred.

What would be a greater sin; going out and using the little piece of this great world that God has created to manufacture some kind of reactionary response in ourselves, desperately trying to fulfill one or more developmental or experiential insufficiency that we have taken into our selves through either action of our own or those perpetrated against us outside our own active choices? We can do this, oh so often, by fulfilling these soft-spoken desires with just the simplest elements of the complex gift that God has presented before us.

Or, and I believe worse, seeing us missing the ball completely in regards to a particular gift God has blessed us with, out of His most generous graces, just to have us ignore it altogether, mainly because we were to busy stuffing another short-term pleasure in our insatiable gap, then to see the roses we so casually tread on by without even reverent acknowledgment?

Case in point; let us suppose God created everything, and if the scriptures are to be taken literally when Jesus said in Luke 13:34; "... if these should hold their peace, the stones would immediately cry out." God drops blessing upon blessings in our laps throughout every single day, and at the end of these days someone else may ask us; "how was your day?", and all we can casually say is; "It was ok." If we could just stop to hear all the angels watching, I believe the screams would be deafening to what we have missed.

I hear the Voice of God speak softly in my ear; "When someone asks you; How was your day?"

"And you answer; It was ok, hardly remembering but a moment or two of the very last day, you have just demonstrated to Me, and yourself, that you have wasted the gift of an entire day."

"The gift of a day that I have given you, not to mention all of the gifts within the day that I dropped into your lap."

"When I say wasted, what I mean if you failed to discover all of the gifts I had given you, and more importantly any and all messages, teachings, healing's, precious gems I may have had for you, or the world for that matter through you and them."

Are we not called to discover Him in all of His creation?

Ok back to the weekend, so much learning can take place when we sit down and truly discover the gifts in front of us.

And to try to write about every lesson that presented itself would be like trying to describe a flower in its entirety with mere words. We can print an image with words like an artist paints a picture, a mere representation of what he sees in his mind. While the image can be beautiful, bringing understanding to the observer, it becomes but a shadow of the original experience, lacking depth, volume, sound, smell, all of the emotional contact that plays in each and every gift we receive.

So let me give but an image of what was seen his particular weekend of watching;

"Before you can be used to slay demons in others, you must slay your own."

Bottom line we can not come into growth with God, and make a difference in the lives of others, unless we are willing to clean out the cobwebs of our own rooms, making this temple a Holy and presentable offering to Him. That includes being used to our fullest potential or facilitating healing's, teaching, preaching, or merely bring people to the place where they can find it themselves, being a messenger to others.

When we are so busy considering these but small pieces of His creation, worrying about the fragments of this physicality, the concerns we fixate on often every moment, issues that only represent a fraction of the total creation He gives us, we miss the big boat. We not only miss it for ourselves, but we as believers miss it for those brought into our proximity, and ultimately miss it for The Kingdom.

I find myself standing in line at the grocery store, and before me, sits a one-year-old or so child. He is sitting in a grocery cart, and his mother hands him a plastic relish bottle, then proceeds to continue gathering her groceries.

I watch in amazement as the child examines the gift his mother just handed him. Over and over in his hand, he turns the relish bottle, quietly examining, a smile of satisfaction, and joy not only crosses his face but mine as well. There is a peaceful gratification on the face of the child as he holds the precious gift. Precious because his mother, someone who loves him, handed the bottle to him for his discovery.

The child becomes enthralled in the examination of his new find as he turns it in his hand over and over again. He holds it examining every crevice, every contour, the texture shape, and eventually, yes, even the taste as the little precious child places a small corner in his mouth.

Only after minutes of contemplation and examination is the article set aside, result; the child has discovered all there is to know about this particular gift, and it is only then, that he moves on to the next point of interest.

I'm not sure if it is the purity, the sweet goodness of his examination, the honor he pays the giver with a complete examination, or just the peacefulness demonstrated in such a beautiful face, but one thing I do realize is the child's activities are all good, pure, encompass everything that speaks love, gentleness, and most of all the main thought that comes to this father mind; "what a good boy!"

Did Jesus not say; *"come to me as a little child"?*

We miss the supernatural gifts God would have given the Kingdom because we were to busy taking care of earthly things we believed we need.

"Saul, why do you persecute me?" could apply to each of us, as we squander the treasures of the moment. Do we not kill the gifts?

How many times have I passed on a gift from God, just to continue in the indulgence of the world, some useless activity that I happen to be wasting time with?

The glance of a friendly smile from the lonely soul reaching out in desperate need, as I chose not to return even a look. What a fool the angel that may have been looking to give me an opportunity to give. Being too busy to realize how much wisdom that person may have had for me.

The missed opportunity to reach out to someone in need as I cross the street to avoid the homeless child who happens to have fallen. Not realizing by giving we receive, oh so much more.

The Word I could have received had I looked past my ego to think I could maybe receive from someone below my so-called station. Sitting on my pedestal never fathoming the people below that place I felt I had earned, could have had anything for me. All the missed Words!

How many times was I to busy eating, had I opened my eyes and saw the gift in giving, the opportunity to change the world?

How many times did the most significant person in my life walk by, because I was to busy worrying about the few grains of sand I happen to have clenched in my hand?

How many wasted days did I eat, or just casually smoke, or drunkenly drink, or greedily spend, or haphazardly indulge in some sexual form of gratification for myself, lazily sleep, or just lay on the floor and basically give up because I felt sorry for myself, how many perfect miracles of healing did I miss?

How many spiritual beautiful Godly blessings did I substitute for mere physical dirt?

How many perfect loving relationships of lifelong significance did I exchange for a dirty cigarette?

The blessing in every creation, grasp it and discover it before it passes by our view, that is the goal, and in doing so we display the face of a child, the Face of Christ.

Conclusion

Mornings light glistens on the edges of the reality, each of its high-lights themselves presenting upon displaying another of the numerous gifts the God of Life has so graciously given me. For I am but here at this moment to observe each of their slender created hues of a masterpiece design, perfect and balanced they call with whispers of praise; "See me for I exist." Why? But if not for one reason in this moment of time and space, for me alone to see them.

I answered a call to help of a woman who hadn't been out of her home in nearly a year. When I showed up at her house, the prescription I had received was written instructing me as a physical therapist to help this particular patient with her gait strength, stating simply that she needed help with fall risk outside her home.

Before coming I had spoken to her on the phone at which time she was adamant about needing to know the exact moment I was approaching the door, because she stated that she preferred to open the door and allow me to just walk in rather than me knocking or ringing the doorbell for this always causes her to become immediately scared and chances were she would probably not even answer. This was a bit curious, but over the course of thirty years I have seen many such abnormalities, so be it, I did as she asked.

Entering her apartment I was immediately greeted with a sense of home as the soft light and cozy atmosphere she had assembled around her gave the impression of a person who surrounds herself with peace and love, displaying many objects that comfortably speak of a life surrounded by family, children, and goodness. At least that is how it appeared.

I went on to observe that while she held on to various pieces of furniture including the walls, she clearly walked with enough stability that a walker was not even a necessity and that seemed to match the observed placement over in the corner of the room being casually used right now as a coat rack. The majority of the walking she was doing, basically, was holding on mainly for confidence, more so than actually needing to support herself, for the most part, she walked throughout the apartment with good strength and more than adequate balance.

Upon walking up to the apartment I already had an opportunity to observe the outside sidewalks and terrain around the walkways, seeing nothing unusual that might present itself as an irregular or an immediate danger, so I asked her why she didn't go outside. This sweet woman we will call Maxine, quickly stated that she hasn't gone out for over six months now, and probably thinking about it, it might even be close to a year.

You live alone?

My daughter, she says, comes and visits her almost every day bringing her everything she needs and other than her cat, or going to the doctor on occasion, she never ventures outside.

So I asked her, what happened did she fall? But she assured me that she had never fallen outside but got to the point in her existence inside the house where she didn't trust going outside, mainly because she didn't sleep at night and often in the morning she was so tired, her balance was at risk.

I went on to ask her about her sleep and she shared that she had repeated anxiety attacks every night for the last fifteen years, needing at least three sleeping pills to get even a little sleep, this left her often in the morning so tired she could hardly move. Sleeping pills while they allow a person to get what feels like sleep, the body does not come into a place of rest and she was probably experiencing a sort of exhaustion by the early morning.

At this point it was so long since she had been outside, she was flat out afraid of even the idea of going outside. This fear even manifested so much in Maxine that she was not even willing to answer the door, thus prompting her to speak to me on the phone, needing to know when I was going to walk up, because she would have to unlock the door, telling me to let myself in, as she stood in the corner hoping it was actually me entering. The only other person who came was her daughter and she entered in pretty much the same way.

Maxine had allowed fear to take ahold of her world, limiting her to the point where it affected her health. Giving her exercises or instructions to help her get stronger, while it may affect her overall balance, resulted in nothing more than placing a bandage on a bug bite but letting the bug remain. And since she had no clear deficit, except possible fear, this would only amount to providing her a sort of home personal trainer, something her insurance clearly discouraged.

I suggested if she wished to solve her problem of not being able to go outside she must conquer her fear. She was willing to try but clearly stated her doctor had told her years ago that there was nothing she could do about the anxiety attacks and she just needed to learn to live with it.

"Start the program; turn on the light, find out where the

attack is coming from and close the window."

We set up a scenario where she imagined an onset of fear, by describing someone coming in the middle of the night and suddenly knocking on the door. This immediately precipitated the same fear reactions she felt at night, but with this exception, we went through a practical and useful solution, in this case, I knocked on the door and she told the person knocking to go away or she was calling the police!

We knocked again on the door, she commanded the person to leave in a clear loud voice, and her own fear again left! I knocked again and told her this time just tell the fear to leave. The fear immediately left again.

After the third or fourth time I said; now I am going to open the door and we are going to go outside when you feel fear tell it to leave! She said she would try. We opened the door she immediately said; "Leave!" looked at me with a smile and stepped out through the door.

She promptly turned to me and asked if she needed her walker? I asked; "Are you afraid you are going to fall?" She shrugged and I said; "Tell the fear to leave!"

She did and smiled and started walking down the walk. We

walked up and down the sidewalk for the next twenty minutes and then back to her apartment, in which I hugged her for everything she taught me and said I will see you in two days for your next visit. If you want we will work on your anxiety attacks!

The daughter called the next day asking what did I do for her, what exercises did I give her because her mother had been calling everyone she knew asking them to come over and walk with her outside, not even wanting to take the walker. I told the daughter, to be honest, I gave her no exercises at all.

The next visit I asked her if she still wanted to work on the anxiety attacks, she said maybe but she didn't think it would help, the doctors said there is no cure for anxiety.

"You still pay that doctor," I jokingly said? "Anybody who tells you there is nothing they can do for you but you still pay them or keep going to, seems to me is like going to a mechanic with a funny sound in your engine, being told he can't fix it, pay him anyway and then keep going back for the same advice?"

She laughed.

So what shall we do about these anxiety attack?

"Find out where the attack is coming from, pick up a weapon and fight."

I went on to say; "let's examine what happens the next time you have an anxiety attack because we need to find out what is going on?"

"Perhaps it would be best to leave the room go into another room, and do something that will inject goodness into all of your senses such as read a book, pet the cat, eat a chocolate, whatever, do something good that fills your eyes, ears, and senses with goodness, and I believe you will scare away the anxiety attack."

"But do me a favor, take a small paper and write down exactly what you were thinking about, feeling, or experiencing no matter how insignificant at the very moment you first started to feel the anxiety come on or the moment you wake."

She quickly said; "I don't need to write it down, because I can tell you right now what it is. It is the same thing I was thinking at the moment of ever anxiety attack I have experienced for the last fifteen years. It is always the same."

"I worry about my son. His wife is a witch and she hates me so much she refuses to allow me any contact with my grandchildren."

"Window found!"

"Does your son know you've been waking up every night worrying about him?"

"What, and pile my problems on his already huge pile of problems?" she almost angrily snaps back at me.

"I'm not saying you should tell him, I am merely wondering if you have told him?"

"No, and I'm not going to, he has enough to worry about himself. He is such a pussy when it comes to his wife, he won't do anything about it anyway. She has on multiple occasions told him if he doesn't do exactly what she wants she will take the kids and leave."

"Attacking creature and direction of attack identified!"

"So you have this worry, and there is nothing you can do about it, basically you just take it year after year."

"I guess?" she says with little more sadness then expressed a moment before.

"Close the window, clean up the mess."

"This is what I want you to do; forgive your son for being a pussy and not standing up to his wife for what is right. Even if it is mouthing the words, say them anyway, out loud so you can hear them yourself."

She did.

"And now most importantly, forgive yourself for being a bad mother, raising a pussy son, just taking it, or whatever else that relates to you having to suffer from this issue for so long. Say I forgive me."

She did with a bit of smile.

"Tonight as it gets later pick up a book, something good, read it, maybe a warm glass of milk or camomile tea, something soothing instead of sleeping pills. Drink a lot of clean clear water all day to flush your system, remember to bless the water with thanks each time you drink. Trust me it helps, and I will call you in the morning."

The next morning I called her and she immediate cried out; "wahoo, I had my first full restful nights sleep without pills and any anxiety attack in fifteen years."

I checked on her a week later, she was still sleeping good, walking outside and having fun telling others her story about how she was cured of something the doctors told her was incurable.

She thanked me over and over, even though I tried to assure her; "Don't thank me, thank yourself for having the courage to face the attack, thank God."

"Thank God," she said.

ABOUT THE AUTHORS

Peter Colla, the author, is an American born, European trained practicing Physical Therapist, Artist, Writer, Husband, and Father. Whether it was the fact that he sustained a life-threatening infection of which he was miraculously and completely healed from, one that nearly resulted in the loss of his leg, or the fact that his father contracted MS when he just started studying medicine, he was prompted to study physical therapy, return to America, and practice for over thirty years. Recently married to Anna Colla, the Co-Author and Muse, a European born, practicing International Entertainer, Dancer, Pilates Instructor, Motivational Speaker, wife, and mother, has joined him in an east meets west examination of the spiritual elements surrounding healing. Together they form a powerful two become one team designed and empowered to demonstrate the faithful gifts all of us can enjoy when we look first to God for our healing, health, and wellness. Recently they formed GEMS of Health and Wellness to bring the many treasures, experiences, and gems of wisdom they have been so freely given to anyone who wishes to try.

Two ends of the earth, two philosophies of treatment, East meets West in this practical examination of the Body, Mind and most importantly Spirit, in the form of Belief, all seemingly missing, at least in part in today's medicine. In a conversational format with God, our authors have chronicled observations, and revelations to help individuals be free of the chains of sickness, injury, doubt, and hopelessness.

Over ten years in the making, a practicing medical physical therapist joins with a spiritually guided Pilates instructor and fine arts dancer, teaming up in the holiest union to examine the correlations between Godly healings and medical expectations of today. Both of them experiencing personal miracles of healing in their own pasts, as well as the many they have witnessed since drives them to search for the missing elements in medicine that seem to stimulate miraculous recovery in people not only in the faith environment but naturally all over the world today.

Look with us as we reexamination of the factors of Body, Mind, and Spirit with simple and understandable illustrations outlining successful treatment models, and the assimilation of a workable guideline for people to use for themselves as a means for them to receive total miraculous healing, regardless of their religious or philosophical bias. This quest has put all of us on a path that allows anyone willing to open up and examine the correlation of today's medicine, with the more physical therapy like, as well as natural holistic healing arts demonstrated and documented nearly two thousand years ago by the man who no one doubts to be the most successful healer in the history of the world; Jesus.